1/4   CATS   OP   695

THE COSMOPOLITAN CAT

BEULAH ROTH

The Cosmopolitan Cat

WITH PHOTOGRAPHS BY
SANFORD ROTH

Doubleday & Company, Inc., Garden City, New York

For SANDY
my husband
who was an Honorary Cat

CONTENTS

LIST OF ILLUSTRATIONS

FOREWORD

I speak with some authority when I say that my sister is a kook. Overlaid on her native intelligence and her total recall is a mad passion for animals. It is not for nothing that, as a child, she was known to all of us as "Beulah the horse kisser."

Her love was not confined to horses (it still continues, even though last summer she was bitten by a policeman's mount in Piccadilly and was given first aid in Fortnum and Mason). In the early days, in Prospect Park in Brooklyn, she fell in love with squirrels, chipmunks, and lambs. When we "went to the country" she extended her libido to include cows, bulls, and especially goats. But it was on our excursions to the Bronx Park Zoo that she really demonstrated her full fix. By the hour, she'd watch the leopards, the tigers, and the lions—and I must say, for the record, that they would watch her too. I do *not* believe her when she insists they spoke to her.

Her background and heredity are bare of any affinity to Africa or Asia; she is not in any way related to Edgar Rice Burroughs—and yet the cat family has found in her its staunchest ally. Beulah has concluded an *entente cordiale* with all cats.

She will tell you herself that she's had fourteen cats in her life—fourteen that she *owned,* that is. There are thousands more who are her friends. Have you ever been troubled by the screeching and wailing of frustrated tomcats at night? Have you ever thrown shoes or bottles? If you have, you will not believe that all Beulah has to do is say "hush." To get them to come to her, she makes a faint hissing sound, and instantly they surround her, knowing they are truly loved. I don't explain it; I only report it.

Over twenty-six years ago, Beulah was married to another cat lover, Sanford H. (Sandy) Roth, who was a photographer with a special eye for artists, and you may see some of his sensitive work in these pages, and a great deal more in a book he did with Aldous

Huxley called *The French of Paris*. Beulah provided the captions to the pictures because she always worked with Sandy, selecting subject matter, persuading reluctant children to pose, and interpreting French and Italian for Sandy, who had neither the time nor the will to learn either language. That meant they had to travel together. From 1945, despite the fact that they owned a house in Beverly Hills, they spent most of each year abroad, and it was almost impossible to find out where they were—sometimes Japan, sometimes Africa, more frequently Paris and Rome. They traveled as the mood struck them, or because *Harper's Bazaar* suddenly wanted them to photograph Maria Callas or the gypsies in an obscure corner of France. You could find them in Colette's apartment, in the Palais Royal, or with Cocteau in the South of France, or with Jimmy Dean, who shared Beulah's love of cats, or Vlaminck, or Picasso, or Dufy, or Braque, or Cary Grant, or Anna Magnani, or with Freddie Zinnemann in Australia doing *The Sundowners*.

Wherever they went they tried to take their cat. They succeeded more often than they failed.

Beulah kept copious notes and this book is the result. It will be very helpful to you if you are a photographer's wife with a cat, traveling from Australia to England, to France, to Spain, and to Africa. Oh yes, and Des Moines.

LEONARD SPIGELGASS

THE COSMOPOLITAN CAT

CHAPTER ONE

The
Training
Table

I had intended to call this book *If a Cat Answers—Hang Up*
—but everybody says it's too frivolous a title. It isn't intended to be.
On the contrary, it's factual; it means exactly what it says. If you
ever call me up, hear the receiver lifted off the hook, and then a
faint miaow, it's because Louis, my Siamese cat, has answered the
phone.

For years the sound of a telephone bell has irritated him. By a
process of logic, hitherto known only to leopards, he discovered
that, with a sweep of his paw, he could knock the receiver from its
cradle and stop the ringing. No matter how long the cord, no matter how deviously I hide the instrument, he finds it and says his
equivalent of "Hello!" Do you wonder that I love him?

The first time I saw him he was chasing four of his brothers and
sisters around the brim of a Mexican sombrero.

His name then was Pedro, his two sisters' Estella and Carmen, his
brother's Manuel. Even then, at the age of four weeks, he was perfectly formed—no kink to his tail, eyes evenly matched in focus,[1]
a mushroom-colored coat tinged with the palest taupe around the
ears and legs, the symbol of *bon goût*. Much later, when his color-

---

[1] We must face the fact that Siamese cats "often have kinky tails and cross-eyes, de-
fects which breeders have not been able to eliminate from the strain," or so the
Encyclopaedia Britannica says. "The head is rather long and pointed, the body also
elongate, the hair sleek and short, and the eyes blue. The general color is cream
or buffy, with the face, ears, paws and tail dark chocolate-colored in a variety in
which the eyes are yellow."

ing was fully developed into an elegance, without ostentation, a French painter said of him, "He is made of Braque colors!" The painter was Georges Braque, who disliked all cats in general, and Siamese in particular.

I, on the contrary, dote on cats, so I bought Pedro on sight for twenty-eight dollars, and named him Louis XIV, because he was the fourteenth cat in my life[2] and the first Siamese.

Sir Compton MacKenzie, president of the Siamese Cat Club of the World, was once asked if Siamese were different from other cats. "They only seem so," he said, "because you *pay* for them!"

Wrong, Sir Compton. There *is* something about the Siamese which fires the imagination of their owners—probably the beloved legend that they are derived from monkeys and gazelles.

Kay Thompson, the tall, thin, graceful author of *Eloise*, believes implicitly in the legend, and goes even further. Fascinated by the coloring of Fenice, her pug, so much like that of a Siamese, Kay evolved a theory that the pug's origin is the saber-toothed tiger and certainly oriental. Shave a Pekingese and you have a pug. Using that as a point of departure, she cited all the animals who are subtly colored from beige to brown: the Burma bull, the Siamese, the Burman cat, the Pekingese, and various assorted antelopes and goats. "Why? Why? Why? Why are they like that?" asks Eloise. "They are all," says Kay, "cousins, cousins, cousins."

People who have pets and are at the same time cursed with an insatiable wanderlust are all cousins, too, for together they face, too often, the seemingly insurmountable problem of "take 'em or leave 'em." I have seen many gallant travelers who threw caution to the winds and departed from home, animal in hand.

Once, in Paris, on Avenue Kléber, in a Buick with a Brazilian license plate, I saw a rhesus monkey dressed in pink velvet asleep on the back seat. Such a sight is rare even in Paris, but when a Buick and a monkey come all the way from Rio de Janeiro, it takes on the proportions of a once-in-a-century miracle, rather like finding a truffle under a chestnut tree on the Champs Elysées (which I once did).

Another time in a small hotel in Montparnasse, I investigated a strange hoarse chirping which came from the room next to mine. I

[2] For the record, the others were Twinkle, Pussy Purr-Mew, Pixie, Toby, Zuleika, Linseed, Max, Porgy, Bess, China, and Louis XI, XII, XIII.

suspected a canary with laryngitis, certainly not two caged marmosets arguing over a *croissant*. Their carrier was labeled and tagged by steamships and hotels from Saigon to Miami. Home port: Madrid.

Nothing so odd about that. After all, the Romans took Egyptian cats back with them as war souvenirs. Some cats joined Cleopatra's navy and got to Japan a thousand years later. Many stayed on shore after the ship's whistle blew and made themselves indispensable to the Japanese. (Mice like rice, you know.) Caesar's legions adopted whole families of cats when they crossed the Pyrenees to conquer Gaul, which at that time was divided into three parts. The cats who liked the climate in two of the parts stayed; others waited a few centuries for the Norman invasion and crossed the Channel to England. There they found a welcome hearth and saucers of Devonshire cream, and remained to populate the British Isles with a race of exceptionally robust tabbies.[3]

There isn't a ship afloat today from the rust-scarred tanker to the elegant transatlantic liner which doesn't have at least one cat signed on. The *Queen Elizabeth* has about twenty in her crew, the *Ile de France* and the *Liberté* used to have twenty-six. The new *France*, despite its mouseproof plastic fittings, certainly must keep a skeleton squad of ten to protect its stores of Camembert and Brie from the rodents who have greedy palates for unrefrigerated *fromages*. I'm not so sure about British cooks, but no self-respecting French chef considers a galley a kitchen unless a cat or two is underfoot while he is stirring his *sauce béarnaise* or filling his *vol-au-vents*. A cat on a ship is a symbol of good luck, not bad, as that silly old wives' tale would have you believe. A sailor doesn't trust a ship which a cat deserts; he knows only too well that when a cat's eighth sense tells him to stay ashore there's bound to be trouble on the Spanish Main.

Most cats *do* stay ashore. The modern city cat seldom leaves home. Given proper accommodations—sandbox and litter, chopped chicken livers and South African lobster tail, he will see no reason

[3] The Encyclopaedia Britannica points out that "tame cats from Egypt were imported into Italy at an early date by Phoenician traders and became established long before the Christian era. Their progeny spread over Europe, more or less crossed with the indigenous species. Remains of cats found in Roman villas at Silchester and Dursley are probably referable to the domesticated breed. The earliest record in Great Britain dates from about A.D. 936 when Howel Dda, prince of south central Wales, enacted a law for their protection."

to forsake his sunny window sill until St. Gertrude[4] summons him. Occasionally there is a trip to a summer cottage—this usually in a burlap bag to numb his sense of direction and nullify his ability to establish surroundings, should he be bored by Westport and choose to make his way back to Fifty-first Street. Given a chance, he will. He's a homebody and really couldn't care less about travel. I, on the contrary, am a mover. Since I love Louis with a neurotic passion, I have to take him with me. Since he loves me in return, he agrees to go.

Once I made the original decision to take Louis along, wherever and whenever, I found no encouragement in cat manuals, and certainly none from my veterinary. I was warned about the delicate machinery in a cat's stomach, the multiple possibility of strangulation, drowning, poisoning, and traumas, both for me and for him. Frustrated by all of this advice, I made my own decision from the available alternatives left to me: the probability of Louis dying of grief in a cattery or dying of rage at a sudden Citroën horn on Boulevard St. Germain. Since everybody knows all good cats go to Paris when they die, I chose the latter.

And I began the training the day I got him. At the outset, let me make it clear that there's no sense trying to start to travel with a settled, grown cat. By the time he's a year old he's too inured in his ways to start a new life. You must begin with a kitten. And this applies to all breeds of cats. There are people who suggest that one kind of cat is more adjustable than another. I don't agree. I've had them all and, while they differ in degrees of temperament, they are all basically cats.

For instance:

1. The alley cat. While his immediate antecedents may be unknown, he goes right back into the jungle for his instincts and ability to survive. You will find he is difficult to domesticate, because he has a deep passion for freedom. Thus, at best, a spotty traveler.

2. The Persian cat. He looks like a darling, soft ball of fur, but he has a very bad temper. I wouldn't travel with him if I were you, because he needs so much brushing, and you'll spend most of your time trying to get rid of the fur balls that plague him.

3. The tabby cat. You can get him in almost any striped pattern

4 St. Gertrude of Nivelles is the patroness of travelers, noted for invoking against mice and rats.

that you wish. He's a darling, loves to be loved, is rather a sybarite, and really hates going places.

4. The Manx. He's a nice kitty with soft hair like rabbit fur. Because he has no tail many people think he's related to the rabbit. You won't find many of them around—and if you have one, find him a wife and mate him. They go for rather a high price, except on the Isle of Man, where they're as common as alley cats here.

5. The Abyssinian. Each one of his hairs is ticked with three bands of color. He's a monumental egotist, and rather a favorite of the Argentinians. At least the only Abyssinian cats I've ever seen are owned by Argentinians, and they seem to like to travel in Rolls-Royces.

6. The Burmese. Oh, these are darlings—the friendliest and most placid of cats. But they're very hard to come by.

7. The Maltese. Lots of people call him a blue cat—the siblings may be any color of the rainbow. He loves love and he'll be happy anywhere you are.

8. The tortoise-shell. I've just discovered something about him. *He's* always a *her.* There are no male tortoise-shell cats—and I haven't the foggiest idea why.

In any case, whether your cat is alley, Persian, tabby, Manx, Abyssinian, Burmese, Maltese, tortoise-shell, or Siamese, and you want to take him traveling, you should get him as a baby. The first six weeks of his life are like the six weeks of any infant's—milk and cream and love and warmth, and constant care against distemper and colic. But as soon as he gets his first teeth he's ready for his first lessons.

You can begin feeding him meat. It comes as no surprise to him, because he's born with an inherited knowledge of its flavor, texture, and purpose. All the difficult stages human babies go through to breach the distance between suckling and sitting down to a thick steak are eliminated by cats. But he must also continue to have milk and I find—though many veterinaries[5] disagree with me—that whole cow's milk usually results in distress and a need for burping.

Cats' mother's milk has its closest counterpart in goats' milk. Unless you want to find a wet-nurse cat, you'd be wise to find a source of goat's milk. It'll stand you in good stead, because it's sold all

[5] I have the greatest respect for vets, but, outside of serious illness, you'll have to find your own way.

over Europe and the Orient. Here, at most supermarkets you can get it in a can. You'll have a pleasanter cat with a sleeker coat if you take the trouble to find it.

You also have to find something to replace the cat's mother. Improvising foster mothers for kittens is something of a fine art. I'm told, though I've never verified it, that Pamela Mason wraps a ticking alarm clock in a heating pad, and the kitten swears it's mother love.

I've a friend in Kentucky who stuck four dolls' nursing bottles into last year's squirrel muff. She filled the bottles with canned goat's milk, warmed to cat body temperature, and the kittens cozily sucked away. A cat psychoanalyst may suggest this can lead to an Oedipus complex,[6] but my friend simply insists that it leads to contented kittens.

Once weaned, kittens like to eat often, five or six times from early morning until late at night. Their appetites seem to be insatiable at this pre-adolescent stage, so take advantage of their gluttony by offering them the proper foods for building up those little bones and muscles. A foundation built at this time should insure your cat a long and happy life, providing, of course, that he doesn't fall into one of those malicious traps in this non-catproofed world.

As with a baby, it's mostly a question of vitamins and a planned diet—but it's also a question of a cat's palate—and you can spoil a cat very easily in his early period. And don't think you won't, especially if he's a Siamese. There is a kind of supercilious dignity to a Siamese that makes you want to please him, and you go off scurrying for something that will titillate him. You'll discover that he likes cracked crab, shrimp (deveined), some baby foods, lamb kidneys, and South African lobster tails. The thing to do, of course, is to order all these delicacies (except the baby food) for yourself and give him the leftovers. Only millionaires would dream of buying these things specifically for a cat—only millionaires or insane people like me. I must say in my own defense that I sought as wide a variety of foods to please as I could, so that, on his travels, I would never be restricted to a special and unobtainable diet.

Let me add parenthetically that it isn't the cat's fault if you pamper him. It's your own. It is you who have taken him away

6 Even when you have a mother cat, she gets bored nursing her children and is out looking for another new and exciting lover. So you'd better have a muff around just in case.

from his jungle; you have to pay for it. If you know anything about the major cat family, you'll discover that your own cat is a lion in miniature. He sleeps after he eats. He can have a hearty meal at home and appear at a neighbor's back door five minutes later with a forlorn starving-pussy-cat look—the way his lineal forebears will go from one dead jackal to another. I suspect that cats stock up on food against the day when there will not be any. A cat can go for days without food, but I'd jump clear when you finally put some before him.

All of these, of course, are minimum training steps that can be worked out in the first six months. On the day Louis attained puberty all the muffs and goat's milk and lobster tails came to an abrupt end and he and I went into rigorous training for the Grand Tour.

I began by introducing him to a collar and lead, a feat, I might add, comparable to fitting an unbroken Palomino to saddle. A collar and leash are only safety devices, a modified seat belt. Leading a cat is an optical illusion; *you* go where the cat goes or not at all, and you'll find yourself in some pretty outlandish places. It doesn't take too long before a cat discovers that some collars are easy to shed. He uses a few Harry Houdini twists and turns, and out of the collar he comes. A harness is even easier for him. By backing up into just the right position, Louis slides right out of the confining straps, as I do out of a girdle. The solution is to make sure the collar is leather and a smidge too small. Any sort of leash sold for small dogs can be used for a cat, but I found that the thin leather ones not only work better but provide less temptation to chew than the nylons. (*I* don't chew leashes; Louis does.) A thin chain, I suppose, works, but somehow it's so chichi, though rather impressive in a car.

A collar and leash are essential if a cat is going to be a back-seat driver. He must be under control at all times. You must know where he is. It is very heartening to be sure that he is never more than a leash length away. Usually a cat will curl up next to you, but if he seeks the floor boards, make sure he doesn't fall asleep on the accelerator.

Putting a pussy cat into a car for the first time is a calculated risk; both of you are subject to hysteria, nervous prostration, heading for the hills through an open window, and *mal de voiture*. Because of his inherent good sense, Louis took an intelligent attitude toward

the car. He assumed it was only a house on wheels, fitted with two
sofas and a nice window sill. Within ten minutes he had found his
place between my husband and me on the driver's seat, and, as an
alternative, took over the ledge of the rear window. The leash was
lengthened by adding another to it, so that I could be sure he was
still with us. But after a few months even one leash proved unnecessary. He behaved beautifully and accepted the car as just another silly invention which he had to endure for his owners' sake.

An automobile, if a cat can tolerate one, is the nearest thing to
cat heaven. Cadillac, Volkswagen, Citroën, Rolls-Royce, or jalopy,
they're all the same to a cat. The sun is there when he wants it, on
top of a valise or a tweed coat. There is a dandy substitute hearth
in that cozy little spot under the front seat where the heat comes
up from pipes and exhaust. For sight-seeing, the rear window is a
veritable Astra Dome. For just plain hiding and getting away from
it all, there are chasms and black airless holes between the duffel
bags and valises. I recommend a car every time, but I won't put a
cat into an open sports car because I won't ride in one myself.

The only thing that gave me one of my more durable neuroses
was Louis's reaction to street noises. You can't blame the cat if he
shows signs of battle fatigue when he is awakened from a deep
dreamless sleep by a passing diesel truck. Vespas and Lambrettas
made him cringe; Cadillacs and Thunderbirds were his mortal enemies and he hissed and spit at them if they ever tried to pass us.

Now, ten years later, Louis is still sensitive to noise, but he has
learned to control himself. After countless miles and kilometers in
our Buicks, Citroëns, Jaguars, and Mercedes, he ignores other cars.
A Greyhound bus with an overcharged exhaust, his former number-
one enemy, is as inoffensive to him as the vacuum cleaner at home,
his former number-two enemy. Nevertheless, there are a few noises
that still make him unreasonable: inflating tires, pneumatic drilling,
electric razors, mixers and blenders, the toot of a ship's whistle,
snapping fingers. It was easy to eliminate most of the annoyances
by avoiding the occasion of sin: keeping Louis off streets that were
being paved, having our tires taken care of when he wasn't with
us, shaving with an old safety razor, and mixing cakes and milk
shakes by hand. The ship's whistle, alas, was out of our control.

On our twenty-five-day journey from Los Angeles to Le Havre on
the French freighter *Winnipeg*, high noon was announced every
day by a soul-shattering blast. The *Winnipeg*, being a small ship,

had few places that were out of range of this nerve-racking noise. After four ghastly days at sea I discovered a perfect solution. At five minutes before noon I deposited Louis and myself in our little bathroom, closed the door, turned on all the spigots in basin and tub, and as my watch ticked toward one minute before noon, I gave the convenience a hearty flush. The bathroom was as humid as a jungle, but utterly insulated by a wall of sound. High noon, with its fanfare, came and went, and Louis never knew otherwise.

But a cat cannot always be coddled by plumbing, and must learn to accept life and face up to the fact that the world is larger than his own house and car. He must condition himself to the grisly knowledge that there are many people in the world who have scents and smells, sometimes delicious, sometimes not. He has to learn that some humans ignore him, some are afraid of him, some love him—even though they stroke his coat the wrong way. (Down to the tail. *Never* up. Please!)

Thus the training for Behavior in a Public World must be carried out in public: department stores, post offices, and shops. Best to find a friendly shop owner like my dear friend Marian Hunter, who sold books in Beverly Hills. Marian allowed Louis to browse among the fiction and cookbooks, to sit on her cash register, and to meet the customers. It did Louis a world of good and lost Marian only a very few customers.

Department stores offer a variety of seminars in public cat behavior. For these forays, I'd let Louis sit on my shoulder, his leash tightly held in my hand, as control against his natural appetite to ravage the nylon stocking department at Saks, or nibble the flowers on Hedda Hopper's hat in the elevator at Magnin's (she was darling about it), or worse, scratch the arm of a child and bite her mother's leg in the May Company. (They threatened suit, but I settled the case with chocolate sodas, and the four of us became the closest of buddies.)

The only time we were asked to leave a department store was when Louis insisted on accompanying me to the hairdressing salon at Saks. There the now familiar sign to all *dog* owners was posted almost invisibly on the wall. Technically, Louis was *not* a dog, but the California law that prohibits dogs from entering all markets, restaurants, and beauty salons encompasses cats too—*and* marmosets—*and* skunks—*and* gibbons—*and* alligators. If they mean *pets*, why don't they say so? Dogs were the real culprits that made such an ordinance necessary with their endless leg-lifting and their penchant for sniffing and snooping at the wrong things.

Now, I love dogs, especially a sober Welsh terrier named Macoco whom my brother considers the King of All Dogs, but even he is quite a different matter from Louis. Dogs are not serene and introspective; cats are. Dogs are outgoing and objective; cats are withdrawn and intellectual. Dogs *obey;* cats *consider.*

That's why it's possible to travel with a cat. As for people who travel with dogs—well, I'm as fair and open-minded as the next one, but *really* . . . !

CHAPTER TWO

Transportation

I've had to hold many street-corner conferences on how and *why* I travel with a cat. Don't they quarantine them? Is it hard? Is it easy? How do you feed them? How and where and when do they do what comes naturally? Isn't it a bore?

No, it's not a bore, not if you're going someplace to *stay*.

If you're going on a cruise or a Cook's tour, leave your cat home. It's not only a bore; it's forty kinds of hell.

With four hours to explore Paris, thirty-five minutes at Pisa, a full hour at St. Peter's, and less than two days in Antibes, a cat makes a repulsive traveling companion. Just finding fresh meat or some sawdust for his box will take up most of your precious time.

Our sojourns in Europe were for working purposes, and wherever we went, we stayed from four to nine months, either in an apartment or so comfortably established in a hotel that Louis, my husband, and I all felt we were in Beverly Hills.

In order to travel you and/or your cat must board some moving vehicle which will remove you from your version of Beverly Hills to those wide unknown spaces known as The World. For this purpose we will consider the automobile, the bus, the train, the plane, and the ship, or a fitting combination of all five.

The train and the bus are known as *public conveyances* and therefore have a stack of not-to-be-broken laws about animal passengers. The bus is *so* public that I wouldn't recommend it as a means of transporting a cat unless it's for a very short journey and in dire emergency. Coach trains come under this same heading; if you can't afford a bedroom, leave your cat at home. Both of these public transportation conveyances demand that your cat (or dog or alligator) be incarcerated in a carrier. Such a carrier, whether it be an old-fashioned champagne basket or a new-fashioned quonset hut made of transparent plastic, will have your cat yelling for food, his sandbox, or just some civilized conversation. Since a cat can't settle down to a good Ellery Queen mystery, he may get very bored and *loud*. Take a portable radio along and then turn it up *louder*. The only proper use for rock and roll music is to drown out a cat's protests. Sometimes it's hard to tell which is which.

On American trains, *if* you've splurged and bought a bedroom, compartment, or drawing room, you can do without the radio and keep your cat with you, but the doors must be closed and left that way. Porters making up berths are your only real threat. Be sure George knocks, then tip wildly and ask him to allow you to occupy an unused room until yours is ready for occupancy again.

On continental trains (the European continent, of course), don't risk buying a wagon-lit unless you are traveling with your husband or lover,[1] or have paid for the use of the entire compartment, *or* have specified that you want one for single occupancy. They do have them, and I advise it because once I boarded the Rome–Paris Express and was rejoicing in the luxury of a solitary compartment, Louis lying on the ugly brown blanket that covered me as I tried to read myself to sleep, when the train stopped at Milan to pick up some random passengers. One of them was destined to be *my* room-mate. Although he was an Italian of the Rossano Brazzi type, not too old or too young, I was appalled at having to spend a night in a room alone with a strange man. *Grâce à Dieu*, he *hated* cats!

European trains make no charge for animals unless they travel by freight. I don't mean all trains—actually, the Rome–Paris Express does make a charge. I did not pay the first time it was mentioned to me, considering it an affront, but on my return journey the conductor brandished the book of railway rules governing transportation of livestock, monkeys, horses, dogs, and *cats*. The rule is fuzzy, especially in Italian. But I paid. Once in Paris, I researched the situation. I know now that keeping Louis in my compartment as a free loader was *not* illegal. The charges noted in the conductor's vest pocket manual were actually for beasts being *shipped by freight*. I wrote endless letters but I never got my money back— and 3800 lire is about $6.25—the cost of a facial.

No worry about a restaurant cat bill, because I always took my

[1] In Europe, wagons-lits are sometimes used instead of motels. And the cat is an excellent cover-up. This is all hearsay, of course.

cat's lunch with me and, let's face it, on some European trains, my own as well. Precaution, that's all. I never knew whether I would be at lunch or dinner during a stop when a fellow passenger with larceny in his soul would enter my compartment and leave the train with Louis, my valises, and even my toothbrush. It's been done, you know! And Louis, fierce as he is, is no match for a persevering robber. So stay with your cat and eat in your room.

A well-tipped porter—and this is international—will attend to any of the little niceties like refrigerating your cat's liver or shrimp until it is needed. On that fine American train, the Super Chief, where you can trust the passengers as well as the chef, I use the dining car. You may be as lucky as I was on one journey: on a westbound trip I ran into a dining steward who was an enthusiastic cat lover. Delighted to have Louis aboard, he served him a complimentary $4.75 sirloin steak cooked to a cat's taste (raw). I had to pay for mine.

The transcontinental trip on the Santa Fe or the Union Pacific has one drawback—that long wait in Chicago between trains. You have to get off the one you're on, but you don't board the other for quite a while—several hours, in fact. So what to do with yourself, and, more important, your cat?

Now, here is where your quonset hut carrying case or your champagne basket or that chic little basket house that Juan built in Madeira comes in handy. Put the cat into it, but first see that he has used his gent's room. It's a long wait, remember. And then check him as you would a piece of baggage. Sounds cruel, but it isn't. Chicago is a notorious stopping-off place for man and beast alike and the checkroom at either station respects the contents of anything that resembles a cat carrier. That's the economical way out, of course. When I'm flush, I take a hotel room and deposit Louis on the bed, his sandbox in the bathroom, with enough food to keep him happy while I visit various odds and ends of aunts and uncles who live in the suburbs. The usual thing is to go to Marshall Field's, but a cat carrier is heavy and a cat on your shoulder while you are browsing around the antique department might turn him into a raging beast and you into a scofflaw. *No* loose cats allowed in Chicago department stores.

As for taking cats into subways, or the Madison Avenue or Wilshire boulevard buses, the drivers couldn't care less when a passenger boards carrying a strange-looking basket with a door and

28 THE COSMOPOLITAN CAT

two holes in it. Ladies' handbags are so weird these days: The
BMT seems to have no objection; neither does the Paris Métro. The
Union Pacific and the Sante Fe nod in approval, and the Paris
Lyon-Méditerranée say, *"Oui! Oui!"* But don't ever try to free-load
a cat on a bus in Madrid!

Now we come to planes—infernal machines, but *fast.* They make
the ordeal of travel much simpler, even though I miss the sheer
thrill of sailing from the Port of New York on the *Liberté* or the
dear old *Ile de France* or the *Queen Mary* or the *Vulcania.* One
airline is the same as another as far as a cat is concerned—he is
just a piece of baggage. All sentiment is ruled out. Only his weight
and the weight of his carrier are considered, and the fare judged
from that. If you send him as unaccompanied baggage, you might
get a better rate, but that may mean a long unthinkable wait for
him alone in some airport until *you* arrive. Better to save money on
something else.

Your cat is weighed in—and this includes cat, everything he has
eaten for breakfast or lunch, and his basket or carrier. I've noticed
around international airports these days many of those wicker car-
riers that are made in Madeira. I'll admit they took chic and certainly they weigh next to nothing compared to a wooden traveling crate, but I'm not too sure about their safety. Mighty crushable
is wicker and so is a cat. The only way to judge a proper case is by
its usability for the cat and you. It's you who will have to carry it
on many occasions. But weight should be the least important detail.
A few pounds more or less add up to an additional expenditure of
nine to fifteen dollars. It's *not* deductible, but then *nothing is too
good for a cat.*

And the best thing is to try to persuade the airlines to let him
travel in the next seat to you in the grownup cabin.

SAS at first seemed to be quite liberal with their offer of permission to do just that. But it's mostly lip service, because they
limit the weight to eleven pounds (cat and carrier). You're in some
trouble unless your creature is a Chihuahua, a Yorkshire, or a kitten
under five months of age.

According to the latest reports from Pan American Airways, they
will allow you to have your cat or whatever with you in your
cabin on international first-class and economy flights, provided, of
course, that you use a carrier and weigh it with the rest of your
hand luggage and pay excess if necessary. Pan Am seem to be

quite liberal as far as pets are concerned, so Mr. Van Horn in the
Los Angeles office informed me. So much of their business is done
with zoos and circuses and white hunters that it's a rare flight that
doesn't carry an elephant, a race horse, a few hundred monkeys, or
a brace of anacondas.

On my first flight with Louis from New York to Los Angeles, I
relinquished him in his carrier at the weigh-in desk. My heart
sank as I saw him disappear into the bowels of Idlewild Airport,
sharing the moving runway with briefcases, hand trunks, Boston
bags, and Grasshoppers. Although he had been tranquilized by a
quarter grain of phenobarbital, I worried about his reaction to a
jet take-off. I worried, too, about the fact that the baggage handlers
who load luggage helter-skelter into planes might not recognize the
cat case for what it was.

By the time we were over Cleveland, I had managed to gather
enough courage to ask the stewardess where they put cats when
they were checked in as baggage. She picked up the phone on the
intercom and spoke to the pilot, then turned to me and said, "It's
too late to do anything about it now, he's in the hold." All I could
think of was a solidly frozen cat screaming through the last
agonies of death, lacerating his feet trying to break out of his box.

The trip to Los Angeles was interminable, despite the three
martinis I accepted from my fellow passengers to quiet my nerves.
The delay at the luggage reception depot didn't help my hysteria
and, when I finally saw the familiar quonset hut case with its labels
and baggage tags, I actually didn't have the courage to claim it.
When I pulled myself together and opened the little wire mesh
door, I was ready to witness a case of cold-blooded murder—or
worse, a cold-blooded cat, but instead I found a very warm one,
a very content one, all purrs and stretches, one who could have
continued on to Jakarta with very little encouragement.

Well, it turned out that they'd been working on planes, no doubt
as a result of so much livestock frozen stiff. In the jets, now, they've
a small section reserved for animals, as properly heated and pres-
surized as the large cabin upstairs. Bless them!

For this service, domestic airlines charge you eighty-eight cents
a pound excess baggage rate for the cat and carrier. My cat weighs
eleven pounds and his carrier six, therefore I pay on seventeen
pounds. International flights collect $2.26 a pound for excess. A
seventeen-pound cat combine like Louis and carrier runs into

the higher brackets. I had considered putting him on a diet a few weeks before such a flight, but chose instead to lighten my own luggage to make up for the deficit. Transcontinental flights, even the Los Angeles–New York hop, are usually never more than five hours. That's perfect cat-nap time. Polar route flights, or what they seem to call polar flights from California to London, Paris, or Copenhagen, are about twice as long—ten and a half to eleven hours. If the airlines keep their word and allow you to keep Pussy Purr-Mew with you, you must put him back into his box at mealtimes.

Having traveled on international air routes at all seasons of the year and by every conceivable route, I would suggest, if you make the trip during the height of the tourist season—June–September— that you go catless. You're bound to have to share your seat with one or two people, depending on your class, who are equally bound to be ailurophobes (cat haters).

If you want to avoid them, go by ship.[2]

The low fares charged for cats on ocean liners is no reflection on their (the cats') prestige. The usual fare for a transatlantic crossing is only ten dollars and the cat can eat his weight in lobster if he cares to. Dogs have to pay fifty dollars and don't eat as well— dog food is all *they* get. On short crossings such as Naples–Capri, Nice–Corsica, Civitavecchia–Elba, there is no charge. I haven't asked about the Channel crossing from England to France because cats or dogs cannot enter England without a six months' quarantine period. (More about *that* later.) On these small boats, actually ferries, it's catch as catch can for the seats. I always took Louis aboard without his carrier, just a leash, to see that he didn't wander into the ladies' room at an unexpected moment. The management of these lines puts you on your honor to see that your animal behaves himself and doesn't attack the other passengers. Continentals take a dim view of somebody occupying a seat for which he has not paid—and this means *you!*

Freighter fares are slightly higher than the average six-day Atlantic crossings. I paid the French Line fifteen dollars for Louis to travel on the *Winnipeg* from Los Angeles to Le Havre, a twenty-five-day voyage. I am sure you could take your cat all the way

[2] The big ships *always* have room for pets, but not freighters. Since they have very little deck space and only take on a maximum of twelve passengers, the number of animals on a voyage is limited to *one*. You not only have to be pretty lucky to get space for yourself; that same good fortune must apply to your cat or dog.

from San Francisco to Brisbane for very little more and you don't have to bring lunch along—your cat is fed the best of everything on the house.

Cats seem to adore ocean voyages, but on the advice of the salty captain of the *Ile de France,* I kept Louis locked in the cabin when I was not in there with him. "Ships are not catproofed," said he. "There is a cat trap every other meter on deck. Open holds, anchor chains, drain-off spouts, smokestacks, high seas . . ." He enumerated about twenty-five terrible things that could happen to cats if they had the opportunity to wander on deck unaccompanied by their owner and held by a leash. As I think back to his list now, I wonder if he purposely omitted the most terrible danger of all—to be mistaken for a rabbit and served as *civet de lapin* for dinner!

I'm in love with the French Line for many reasons, but primarily because of its attitude toward cats. This passion for felines, which is a normal French trait, runs directly through the management of the Compagnie Générale Transatlantique from Guy de Berc, commander-in-chief of North and South American operations, to the enchanting *Garçon de Dogs* aboard the *Ile de France,* the *Liberté,* and now *La France.*

The kennel aboard the French Line ships is situated on the top deck in a specially built enclosure. It resembles a top-drawer boarding kennel, which indeed it is. If the passenger list is full, so is the facility with as odd as assortment of pets as masters. Chows, Dobermans, shepherds, Hungarian pulik, Scotties, and corgis all share this international settlement with a minimum of barking (they're too seasick). Dogs can be promenaded by *you* each day and nobody really cares too much if you forgo the daily movie, Bingo, or horse racing to spend your time visiting your dog. The French Line has a special printed menu for the dogs on board, respecting both American and European tastes in food. (I noticed that the *carte du jour* lacked that added ingredient of "kibble" which adulterates most American dogs' diets.)

Cats are another thing. Technically, they should be placed in the kennel too, *but* it takes only one cat-loving purser to grant permission for you to have Pussy in your cabin, provided, of course, (1) you are alone or (2) accompanied by lover[3] or husband or friend. At the height of the high season it would be a *gaucherie*

[3] Sometimes, instead of motels or wagons-lits, the French use ships. Again, strictly hearsay.

even to ask the purser to allow your cat to share a cabin with you and those inevitable three schoolteachers from Detroit, all quite as inevitably aelurophobes.

Even in low season I always took the precaution of having my door securely closed whenever Louis was left alone. Too, I always remain *in* the cabin while it is being cleaned and vacuumed by the steward. I don't know about your cat, but mine resents intrusions of any kind. Although the stewards are usually kind gentlemen who perform their duties discreetly, a sudden movement with a feather duster or an attempt to remove a food plate is instantly interpreted by Louis as an Act of Aggression. He takes measures that send the stewards flying into the companionway, thus announcing my secret to the ship's company.

You see, nobody ever suspected Louis's presence on board until the steward spread the rumor. Having my cat in my cabin was *my* business, but by the end of a six-day voyage, cat lovers, deprived of their own darlings, came to see and chuck Louis's chin, and gossip. There were so many visitors on one crossing that appointments had to be made days in advance so that my cabin could accommodate Louis's guests.

It was on the dear *Liberté,* just before she went to the junk heap. We had just pulled out of Le Havre when the gongs rang for lunch— *déjeuner est servi!* I was assigned to a table with a nice gentleman from Chicago and a lady who was *so* French: a little-nothing black dress, pearl earrings, divine shoes, hair not too far out or too far in, and a poise unduplicated in any other woman in the world.

I said "hello" and "*bon jour*" and introduced myself to my two companions, who did not know one another. The dining-room steward, who knew me from other voyages, greeted me and asked if Louis XIV were on board. When I assured him Louis most certainly was, he suggested some un-garlicked *gigot* (he knew Louis's aversion to strong flavors), as an homage to him from the *salle à manger,* until other feeding arrangements could be made. My female table companion asked me if my child were ill. Terribly embarrassed, I hesitatingly confessed that Louis was only a cat. My French-speaking table companion lost her poise and shrieked with joy: "A *cat!* What cabin are you in?"

When I told her it was 316 B deck, she screamed again. Hers was right next door. I'm afraid we both deserted the nice gentleman from Chicago and the lovely chocolate soufflé, and headed up a flight of stairs to our corridor. By luck, there was an adjoining door between our cabins. It remained open throughout the voyage and my new-found friend, who was not French but Belgian, has remained dear to me to this day. She was more or less an expert on Siamese cats and keeps from four to six of them on her ranch in the mountains near San Bernardino, California, where, as lineal descendants of St. Patrick, they keep her property clear of rattlesnakes.

It happened to me, so it can happen to you. Once the crew is notified that there is a cat in your cabin, this information reaches the kennel man high up on that windy part of the ship known in brochures as the sun deck. An hour or so after your ship sails, a short man, ageless, smelling deliciously of dogs, knocks on your cabin door to make a list of the foods your cat likes. He assured me that I didn't have to order *only* what Louis liked. It would be just as convenient to order what he *adored*. It made no difference to the French Line if Louis asked for caviar or Nova Scotia salmon, or crab meat, or smoked oysters, or *crème caramel*, or baked Alaska. Actually, Louis liked none of these things, but he did dote on calf's liver, rare roast beef, un-garlicked leg of lamb, or raw *entrecôte*. It was like rubbing Aladdin's lamp. Come high sea or low sea, at eight each morning and six each night there was a hesitant knock at my door—hesitant, not because the *Garçon des Dogs* was afraid of waking *me*, but terribly careful not to disturb Louis. Brunch and dinner were served in the noted French Line manner, on their best Limoges, each portion enough for seven cats, and the temperature and size of the tidbits just perfect for a cat's taste.

I might as well say it here:

> *Darling French Line,*
> *You're the* most,
> *The absolutely*
> *Perfect* host!

A cat has to be exercised even on a ship, but I tried to make it as top secret as possible, choosing those moments when everyone was asleep, playing Bingo, or still dawdling over the last crumb of Roquefort at the dinner table. I walked him on deck as often as I could, but in bad weather I used the desolate public rooms. The potted palms, bay trees, and other seagoing floral décor offered him a chance to sniff growing things in search for a tuft of grass.

His digestion, like that of all oceangoing creatures, depended on the whims of the sea.

A seasick cat is a pretty sad sight, only a little less sad than a seasick human, and a great deal more dignified. Cats have the same symptoms and the same misery, the only difference being that it doesn't show on their faces. They want to be left alone, just like you or me, but enforce it by getting under a bed or hiding in a dark corner. Veterinaries have special motion-sickness pills for cats, so don't dose them with dramamine unless your veterinary says you can. *Mine* says, "No! No!"

Keep all food away from his sight. He'd hate you even if you shoved a mouse under his nose. Liquids are taboo too. They're what probably made him sick in the first place. *If* he is perishing from thirst caused by the dehydrating effect of his nausea, leave him with an ice cube to lick. By all means keep the door to the loo shut. Cats seem to know where to find a dripping faucet or, better yet, the toilet bowl.

I'm not quite sure I mean better yet. I *am* sure the nicest thing about a sea voyage with a cat is Le Havre.

CHAPTER THREE

Bureaucracy

I'm not so sure of that either, because there are landing formalities that are not congenial. Does a cat need a passport? No, but he has to have papers—oh, quite a lot of them.

Even with all the papers, the welcome sign for animals visiting a foreign country can be turned to the wall with an outbreak of rabies. Japan's Department of Agriculture excludes all fauna from entering, *except* cats. Hawaii, the Scandinavian countries, and of course the British Empire, quarantine *everything* as long as it comes under the heading of carnivorous quadruped—and that means cats and dogs.

The British have the most rigid quarantine laws of all. You must leave your animal in an approved kennel or cattery for six months. This law is enforced with vigor wherever the Commonwealth's sun shines. So difficult is the procedure involved in taking a cat or dog into England (or Australia or Canada) that, unless you are migrating permanently, it's better to avoid England, Ireland, Scotland, Wales, Malta, and Gibraltar until the law is repealed. (And I'm working on it.)

But here's how you do it *if* you must. First apply for a license from the Ministry of Agriculture and Fisheries in London. Depending on the Minister's mood, it may take months to get it, or you may receive it in a week. In dealing with Her Majesty's Government, it's best to start long in advance to allow the Tory red tape to untangle.[1]

Once the license is received, you visit the British Consulate nearest your home, where a list of said approved kennels or catteries is

[1] I'm apolitical, so I hasten to add that the cat exclusion law was adopted by a Labor Government, under Ramsay MacDonald. At least, that's what I'm told by Conservatives.

shown you. They are all good (in fact, excellent), but it is advisable to choose one nearest London, or Glasgow, or Cardiff, your own focal point. The consul will also arrange for the paddy wagon to meet your animal at the dock or airport. This doesn't mean that your pet is snatched from your arms and thrown into a dog catcher's cage. The British love them too much for that, but the adieu you say will have to last the whole, heartbreaking six months. (I wouldn't try smuggling Fifi or Michou in either, because the Men in White are expecting you.)

The approved kennel near London accepts both cats and dogs and is the pride of the RSPCA. It is Hackbridge Kennels, London Road, Hackbridge, Surrey, England. You have visiting privileges, of course, but your communication with your pet will be as strictly censored as a visit to an inmate at a state penitentiary. No touching allowed!

You will have to pay for the license, the Black Maria that meets you at the port of entry, and let us not forget the boarding fee.

If you want my advice, let the British keep their cats, and you keep yours—*away*. If you must see the island of Malta, shoot grouse in Scotland, or buy cashmere sweaters or Spode on Regent Street, do it on your own, catlessly.

Britain is not the only country with a fear of cat contamination so, when a forthcoming trip is only a glint in my eye, I quickly call the proper consulate to get the latest news on carnivorous quadrupeds, right from the horse's mouth. France and Italy had always taken a devil-may-care attitude about traveling cats and an inquiry about regulations concerning them usually provokes uncontrollable laughter. A French consular clerk shrieked with laughter at the idea of taking *another* cat to Paris. "Bring in all *les* cats you *voulez, madame!* What is one *plus* cat *en* France?"

Indeed?

On December 7, 1957, an infamous date on a far more important count, the French government put into effect an edict signed by President Coty, specifically barring all *American* carnivorous domestic animals from the shores of metropolitan France. When the announcement was first made on November 29, I was stunned to think that my beloved France could do *this* to me. Then Romain Gary, our French consul, pointed out that it was not exclusively an anti-American law—animals from Spain, Greece, Italy, and Germany were included in this sinister ukase.

That calmed me, until I discovered that animals from the "clean countries" were excepted: Great Britain, Norway, Sweden, Denmark, and of course Switzerland.

Not only was my patriotism wounded, but my travel plans had to come to an abrupt end with a sailing date two weeks away. Louis had many appointments in France with Picasso and Cocteau; now he was a pariah, an untouchable, a leper! The situation proved to be so embarrassing that I decided to take matters into my own hands and find out why the U.S.A. was not considered a *clean country* by the French. I immediately dispatched this wire:

The Honorable John Foster Dulles
Secretary of State
State Department
Washington, D.C.
DEAR MR. DULLES:
It has come to my attention that the French have a new law excluding American, Spanish, Greek, and German carnivorous domestic animals, while no such provision is made in the case of animals from Sweden, Norway, Denmark, and Switzerland. I hope you will make vigorous diplomatic inquiries to find out why American animals are now *persona non grata*, despite the fact that they are properly vaccinated and have created no incidents in the French Republic. I suspect there is a subtle anti-American bias in this, Mr. Secretary, and I know that I speak for thousands of cat lovers, when I urge you to make stern representations to the Government of France.

Almost immediately I received the following letter from the State Department:

DEPARTMENT OF STATE
Washington

In reply refer to
EUR: WE   December 6, 1957

DEAR MRS. ROTH:
Reference is made to your telegram of November 29 regarding French restrictions on the entry of carnivorous animals.
The information available to the Department indicates that the restrictions, which become effective December 7, are intended to assist in dealing with an epidemic of rabies. This information does not indicate that the restrictions are intended to be discriminatory.

Sincerely yours,
For the Secretary of State:
RICHARD M. SERVICE
Deputy Director
Office of Western European Affairs

Well, I could see that diplomatic negotiations would get me no-where—and yet I *had* to take Louis with me. For months he'd been in a bad mood, and he was looking forward to the trip. Well, that isn't exactly true. It's hard to tell what a cat is looking forward to. The truth is *I* had been looking forward to the trip. On top of that, I was to be gone a year, and you can see how impossible it was to leave Louis in a public cattery[2] for all that time. I had to get around the new French law.

Yet its provisions were pure and concise: *no entry*. There were no loopholes left for quarantine, vaccination, or officially stamped certificates from veterinaries.

Having lived in Europe, especially France, for such a long time, I knew that all laws and regulations have an "open door." Some-where there had to be a vulnerable point, a debatable paragraph, a technicality in the legal language, and I determined to find it. Immediately I wrote to the U. S. Public Health Service, the Minis-tère d'Agriculture in France, President Coty, and above all to Jean Cocteau, who, among other things, is president of the Cat Club of France. Monsieur Cocteau was livid but helpless.

Then I wired Guy de Berc, commander-in-chief of North and South American operations for the French Line. He wired back sadly:

> Wish I knew what you can do. Stop. Am barking my head off. Stop. Still expecting some explanation. Will communicate with you later. GUY DE BERC

Then I wrote Art Buchwald. *He* wrote in his column in the Paris *Herald:* "Mrs. Roth set up a howl which could be heard from Los Angeles to the darkest corner of the State Department in Washington."

I wasn't the only one. French consulates all over America were receiving threats from pet owners who warned they would boycott France forever if the law weren't changed or at least loosened. Personally, I made Romain Gary's life impossible. I nagged at him, and I've taken lessons from the best fishwives, until he admitted the French Line and Air France were beginning to lose a great deal of business; *enfin* he gallantly agreed it was about time the

2 The uninformed grin and call these places "cat houses," an obscene circumlocution of which I hope you are never guilty.

French government changed its mind about the validity of a rabies inoculation.

This was the bone of contention. American veterinaries claim that a rabies vaccination will prevent an animal both from giving it and from getting it. French veterinaries claim it prevents the animal from getting it but, *mon Dieu*, can he *give* it! (The French are dead wrong, as Pasteur could have told them.)[3]

My telephone rang steadily for two weeks (the L. A. *Times* was indiscreet enough to do a story on Louis and me) with pro and con cat people advising me what to do. One lady (obviously a Romany) said she had a way for me to smuggle Louis into France through a contact on the east coast of England, a fisherman who would take me secretly to the shores of Normandy any given dawn. Her price was too high. French expatriates, now living in Los Angeles, used many Franco-Gallic five-letter words to order me to keep my *nez* out of French politics. Often the phone would ring and the only answer to my "hello" was, "You *Communist!*" (Rather more of a monarchist, I should have thought.)

The most constructive call was from a lady by the name of Lillian Berk, who calmly suggested, if taking Louis to France was so difficult, why not leave him at home, at Blackford's Hotel for Cats? She recommended it highly. Dismally, I called Mr. Blackford for a reservation for Louis. I also considered an overdose of sleeping pills.

And then the miracle happened.

A motion was made at a crisis meeting of the Chambre des Députés to amend the law to allow American carnivorous quadrupeds once more to see the Eiffel Tower, *if* they were accompanied by their little brass rabies medals and quadruplicate copies of stamped and notarized certificates attesting to their official registration under state livestock regulations, plus a nice little French visa—indeed, an exclusive *animal* visa.

There was one more "little paper" required. France demanded a sworn statement that an animal entering France on the new liberal terms had not lived in a rabies-infested area for six months prior to entry. Now whom do you call up and ask, "Pardon me, but is Beverly Hills a rabies-infested area?" You call up the mayor, that's who you call up, and he says, "Dear me, no!" And you say,

[3] My human doctor says *I'm* dead wrong.

"Are you prepared to swear to it?" And he says, "I'd better give you the Board of Health." And the Board of Health never really thought much about it, and looks up the statistics, and says, "Beverly Hills hasn't had a case of rabies in twenty years, and we *are* prepared to so swear."

Had we lived one block away, Louis would have been out of bounds, because one block away is Los Angeles, and Los Angeles, at the time, was indeed a rabies-infested area. Don't worry. Giant steps have been taken and the scourge has been stamped out. You can take all the Los Angeles cats you want to France, under the new law.

The French Line and Air France insisted I had singlehandedly forced the Chamber of Deputies to act (which is manifestly absurd) but they persisted in applauding my humane efforts to save their business from going down the drain. I was happy as a lark when suddenly a member of the French Consulate called me to warn me that, if I intended to travel with Louis to Spain or Italy, I could not return to France with him because then he would be considered a Spanish or Italian cat. I swore he wouldn't leave France, and I collected my sheaf of papers and took Louis to Paris. It took hours to cross the frontier.

But no longer. Since my run-in with the French government, the laws have eased even further and Louis has been back many times. But bureaucracy is contagious and now Italy demands a great deal of paper work and a great many stamps costing a cat's ransom in lire before the necessary papers are completed for Italian customs and health inspectors. If you are going to Italy, check with the Italian Consulate; the law may be widened or narrowed depending on how an incumbent official feels about carnivorous quadrupeds.

Arriving at an Italian port or frontier with a cat, you may bring out any latent sense of humor the official has been trying to hide for years under his uniform. I always show Louis's documents before I'm asked for them, thereby disarming the official who has that gleam in his eye in the hope that you *don't* have them. The California Livestock vaccination certificate, the gold-stamped notarization on the health certificate, the French or Italian Consulate stamps are considered very impressive. I also have an American Kennel Club pedigree of a dog I used to own, which I flash. It's effective. I watch Louis's papers more closely than my own passport and demand their return as soon as they are read. They always want to keep *something*.

Mostly Louis. They *adore* cats, and laugh gleefully when they see one with a leash and collar. Louis can make the dourest and gloomiest of them bubble. Bored, I assume, by tourists with their endless varieties of gloves, perfumes, cameras, cuckoo clocks, and feelthy pictures, all the members of the *douane* pull the same chestnut when they are confronted with Louis. "Have you anything to declare, Signor Cat?" they ask soberly. "Cigarettes? Cigars? Matches? Radios? Camera? Currency? Hah, Signor Cat?"

They make a pretense of searching Signor Cat's traveling case, and when all they find is an extra leash, a brush, two chipped plates from the Café Select, a tube of Vaseline, and a rubber mouse, they chalk-mark his bag with a great flourish. One wrote on it: "*Amo gli gatti!*"

We might as well finish this little business of non-human passports and international protocol. If you think you've had trouble in Europe or Asia, just wait till you try to take your cat back into the United States.

The United States Public Health Service will tell you, as they told me, that you can take your cat or calf to Rotterdam or Shangri-La, as far as they are concerned, but you had better have your animal's rabies inoculation certificate on your return to the U.S.A. —or else! The "or else," in this case, means a quarantine of from two weeks to eternity until it can be proven that your Puss Puss, Bow Bow, or Moo Moo is pure and unadulterated, especially if he's just come from a country where a rabies epidemic is raging. (There we go again!)

It's so much easier to have your local veterinarian give your cat a vaccination, which is as harmless to an animal as a pat on the back. Cats needs a special vaccine, which is less potent than the one used on dogs, so be sure that your veterinary knows all about cats. Government inspectors may not be so considerate, making an emergency inoculation at a port of entry. The wrong vaccine could prove to be disastrous. Louis is vaccinated regularly each year by Dr. Miller and has a necklace of the little brass tags to prove it. That's only a sensible precaution should he tangle with a rabid rat, a mangy skunk, or even a dog who gets too fresh. Cats bite, like all other animals, and unless you can prove a fresh immunization, your next-door neighbor can have your nice little pussy cat put into the hoosegow for two weeks until he does or does not show signs of being afflicted with this terrible disease.

Uncle Sam has another little favor to ask of globe-trotting pets to protect the unfortunates who have to stay in their own back yards. "Please," he says, "get your beast a complete physical examination before you leave the country from which you embark."

It isn't too much to ask, is it? So off you trot with your pet to a veterinary at least ten days before you leave Paris, Rome, Athens, or Istanbul. As a rule, European veterinaries have beautifully equipped offices with the most *avant-garde* stainless-steel fittings. A professor such as my Paris veterinarian, Dr. Fourneau, makes a definite appointment with you for the examination. The charge is about two dollars for the most complete going over your cat ever had. The doctor omits no crevice or orifice, all thoroughly investigated with flashlight, magnifying glass, and thermometer. When the tail-to-paw search is over, nothing has escaped the doctor. Ostensibly, the veterinarian is looking for a communicable disease such as enteritis, ringworm, or mange, but you always come away from his office with some sage advice about feeding, and the feeling that you are an extremely attractive woman.

When the examination is over (The cat's, of course. How dare you?) you receive a *Certificat de Santé* (Health Certificate), an official document with stamps and signatures which means that your cat has passed *summa cum*. (A 4-F cat or dog will, of course, delay his owner's departure until his health improves.) The document not only looks official, it *is* official, so hold onto it with your dear life as you would your own passport. Without it, you and your cat may have to spend the weekend at a quarantine station.

This lovely citation and the rabies inoculation certificate are handed to the purser of your ship or plane and turned over to the U. S. Public Health Service inspectors who board your ship or plane at the quarantine station on your arrival at your port of entry. This health rule is very *strict,* and it's easier to get away with murder than a sick cat! And you know your cat is sick if:

(a) He needs Carter's Little Pills.

(b) He needs Kaopectate.

I'd advise you to take plenty of both.

CHAPTER FOUR

Hotels,
Mostly French

It was Pierre Monteux, the noted conductor, who, when refused accommodations at a certain Los Angeles hotel because he insisted on sharing them with his poodle, wrote the management a lively letter: he apologized for vulgar and loud members of his own species, those who spilled whiskey on the rugs, let their cigarettes burn holes in the sheets, and wiped off inkstains, lipstick, and cold cream with the hotel towels. He pointed out that these were acts of vandalism of which his poodle was never guilty. The hotel was faintly amused by the letter; the manager managed a thin smile but did not alter his decision. Pierre Monteux's dog stayed home. So did Pierre Monteux.

That hotel is not alone. A great many hotels consider animals third-class citizens. Just mentioning the fact that you have a cat with you in the lobby may cause a minor crisis at the reception desk.

The *grand luxe* hotels in New York will reluctantly take your pets. Others, less *luxe,* will say no, but will. The next step down won't, but the step after *that* will. Anyway, bribery always works.

In Europe too. Of course, there, it's more of a Fine Art, and you have to negotiate a bribe as you do a deal for a Dubuffet. The etiquette of bribery is a required course in Swiss hotel schools; I am an amateur, but learning fast.

Still, I find it politic to phone first and ask the house policy toward living guests who aren't human. If the answer is *no,* or if it seems they've hung up, there is no point in trying to convince

the reception clerk that *yours* is a significantly different case.
(Silly! Convince the manager! You're bribing the wrong man.)

Hotels' particularly stiff attitude toward cats is a result of the
bad reputation they have for destroying furniture. (Equally silly
because, by the result of day-to-day examination, I observe that
it takes an indoor cat about six months to *really* destroy an upholstered chair. Most hotels now, except those in the *grand luxe*
category, use so much plastic and plasticized fabric that cats have
nothing to look forward to when left alone in a room. Chemistry
has finally defeated a cat's claws.)

Those *grand luxe* jobs have cherished clients, with pets, so they
can't refuse you. Certainly the Ritz in Paris cannot openly reject
a cat when the entire world knows that the Duke and Duchess of
Windsor stay there year after year with an incredible number of
pug dogs.

Middle-class French hotels, trying desperately to get high marks
in the Guide Michelin, want to be on their best behavior. They are
determined to keep out riffraff, which, in their book of rules, means
ladies who rarely *sleep* in their rooms, gentlemen who use the telephone too often, couples with no luggage except a *cinq à sept*, and
animals. Really, it's better to live *en pension* than middle class.
Anything is better than middle class.

Still, I know of *two* darling *upper*-middle animal-loving hotels
in Paris. One, the Queen Elizabeth, on Rue Pierre Premier de Serbie,
is a small, rather elegant place with marvelous service, sympathetic
chambermaids, and the most competent concierge in all of Europe.
The Queen Liz, as her clients lovingly refer to her, is around the
corner from the swankier Georges V, a block or two from the best
butchers, and within scratching distance of three divine *drogueries*.
Besides, it's on the *Right Bank*, which immediately gives you and
your cats *status*.

My other favorite hotel, the Lutèce, is much more *bohème*. Its
façade, on Rue Jules Chaplain in Montparnasse, is pure 1927 "moderne." I think there are only forty rooms in the hotel and, as far
as I know, only *two* private baths. You can come down for your mail
in your dressing gown, have huge cocktail parties in your ten-by-
ten room, and play Django Reinhardt records all night.

Actually, the Lutèce loves animals more than its paying guests.
(At one time its unofficial register showed two marmosets, one
dachshund, a pregnant poodle, an anaconda, a turtle, the regular

hotel cat, a stray kitten, and Louis.) Never was there a tactless reference to the sawdust on the floor, the miaowing,[1] or the shaggy heap of an old leather armchair in *chambre* 25 which served as Louis's scratching post for four years. I tried to restore the bloom of youth to it with leather conditioner and saddle soap, but the management waved me away with a good-humored *ça va!* and wrote it off.

Over that period of four years, *chambre* 25 was waiting for us. *Chambre* 25 is *one* of the rooms with private bath, which makes it the royal suite in any other hotel. Anyone installed in room 25 is, by precedent, entitled to service far beyond the call of duty. It is a *prestige* room and so was decorated with more "chic de Paris" than the others. Room 31, which also has a bath of sorts, is a hall bedroom compared to 25. Its décor (No. 25's) is, like the exterior, pure 1927 "moderne," which the French still do so well. It is a room made for sloe-eyed ladies in knee-length skirts with *sautoirs* and Vionnet blouses and deep felt cloches hiding their Dolly Sisters haircuts. By now, *faute de mieux*, the mustard-yellow velvet covers on the twin studio beds, the Edgar Brandt lighting fixtures, the purple and gold wallpaper, and the skyscraper bookshelves have ceased to have any allure. They should be sent to the Flea Market, but they belong to the Lutèce, so out of sentiment or good French thrift they remain.

Entering the room for the first time, my eye caught a huge black hole on one of the yellow bedspreads. Knowing Louis would be blamed for this arson, I officially and forthwith notified the management that it was a burn of long duration and *certainement* not my fault. The concierge made a note in some sort of a ledger and agreed that I would not be held responsible. For many seasons the spreads remained, occasionally cleaned, but never mended. For me, year after year, they spelled home, as did the vintage radio installed so conveniently high on a shelf over one bed. If you got on a chair and turned it on, you always managed to get voluminous static and strains of Radio Luxembourg, but *never* a Paris station.

Recently a friend of mine, intending to be in Paris for a few months and wanting to see this electronic marvel of a radio, asked for and received *chambre* 25 at the Lutèce, at my suggestion. He

---

[1] By this time you're probably annoyed with this spelling. Wouldn't you swear it should be spelled "meow"? But there's no such word, according to Webster's New International Dictionary. It's "miaow" or "miaou," and there's no use arguing.

of course made a point of the cigarette burn and notified the *patron* that, since he did not smoke, the hole was *certainement* not his doing. "Oh, that?" said the management. "Of course, *you* didn't do it. That was done by Madame Roth's *cat!*" What a dour man that *patron* is! But unbribable.

Sometimes hotels charge a very small sum when an animal shares a room with you. In Paris, for instance, it ranges from seventy-five cents to a dollar and a half a day, depending on the *quartier*. This brings up a problem. The hotels are not allowed to have animals so how to charge for them? The Swiss hotel schools have figured this out with aplomb: the fee is absorbed by stamps or mineral water, which somehow mysteriously appear on your bill. Do not question the charges.[2] On no account discuss them with the chambermaid.

For your best friend in any hotel, *anywhere*, is the chambermaid. The ritual of making a maid your blood sister consists of tipping liberally when you arrive. Nothing seems to cement friendship more than dollars, francs, and American Express traveler's checks. (How those girls dote on traveler's checks.)

After you cross *la bonne's* palm with silver, you begin reciting the instructions, which, you warn, must be followed to the letter or you will call the police, or worse, withhold all future gratuities. Always prefixed by a charming "please" or "*s'il vous plaît*," ask if it is possible (and it always *is*) to have your room done in the morning as early as convenient for *her*.

The cleaning of rooms usually begins at 8:00 A.M., which should be fine for you if you are going to Balmain's or the Louvre. (Best plan is to save the Louvre for the times that Balmain is closed.) If you want to sleep late you can always tell her to go away when she knocks, or tell the night concierge that you don't want to be disturbed. Don't worry, you'll never oversleep for an appointment with a cat around. Louis stares you out of sleep, giving you five minutes of grace before tearing the Paris edition of the *Tribune*, which has unfortunately just been slipped under your door.

Once your room is as neat as a pin, bathroom scoured, sawdust swept up, sheets changed, and towels replaced, there should be no reason for anybody to enter. You may go now, after pussy cat is fed and exercised. That means, after you take him for a walk.

---

[2] Another thing *not* to question is the item entitled "*une douche.*" *That* means a shower bath.

Paris swarms with so many cats these postwar years that I advise you to look behind every lamppost and garbage can before you even attempt to walk yours on the street, if only for a hundred yards. Even garbage is scarce these days, and a cat who has the exclusive on restaurants like Fouquet's or Tour d'Argent is not going to tolerate any muscling-in on his territory. If you think your cat can lick a Parisian *chat gouttière*—Yankee Go *Home!*

The best exercise for a cat (and the easiest on your own nerves) is a long walk in the hotel corridor, and some mountain climbing up and down the Grand Staircase. Cats love to listen at other people's doors, sniff the shoes left to be cleaned, stalk a (sometimes imagined and sometimes *not*) mouse, find a view from another window, or nibble the tip of a potted palm. Always keep the leash on (someday, when I've enough courage to discuss exhibitionism, I'll tell you what happened to *me*).

This is game time too (preferably not with psychopaths), and the best toy for a cat is a rolled-up woolen sock. Portable and washable, to the cat it can be male or female, and certainly it serves to disarm the chambermaid who, finding it in a bidet or under the bed, will just think you're pretty careless and not blame the cat. Rubber mice have frightened too many chambermaids even to be considered in traveling. (I wish they'd frighten the man next door.)

If laundry has to be delivered, ask that it wait until you arrive because you're going to be home by noon. Oh yes, you *are!* At best, there is nothing to do on the Continent at noon but eat, so why not pass by your hotel to see how kitty cat is doing? Going back to your hotel to freshen up for luncheon is very normal so nobody will be the wiser if you check on your cat. Go where you will all afternoon, but don't you dare have that *apéritif* at *l'heure bleue* until you've looked in on the by-this-time-miserably-lonely cat, fed him, walked him around the lobby, and thrown him a sock.

Although I bribe them outrageously, I sometimes feel that chambermaids lie to me about anyone entering my room when I am not at home. *Your* chambermaid may be as honest as *Abe* but she must prove it. Test her: leave, as usual, chatting endlessly about your errands and appointment for haircut and shave (for men) or a coiffure at Georges (not for men), a *vernissage* on the Faubourg St. Honoré, a plane to meet, or lunch with somebody from *Paris Match*. All of this is a ruse. Go nowhere. Return when least expected. If, during your absence, someone entered your room un-officially, the telltale signs will be there: a plumber's wrench, saw-dust on the floor (a carpenter), extra towels, or laundry. And you will *certainly* know if the chambermaid has used your room for a rendezvous with the plumber or carpenter. If she has, she's a doxie, and don't trust her. Just bribe her some more. And, from then on, keep your key.

Very often hotels issue only one key to a room and I suspect that the key fits every other lock too. The idea is to deposit yours on the key board in the lobby when you leave, as a signal to the cleaner-uppers and the rendezvousers that the coast is clear.

Ignore the instructions. Keep your key with you at all times. If your room is not available to the maid because she does not have the key, *tant pis!* Better to have an unmade bed and a ring around the tub than a cat who's gone over the hill, and/or valises and personal belongings that are already for sale in the local Flea Market. (I once bought back a cigarette case at the *Marché aux Puces,* two years after it had been stolen. I *know* I should have gone to the police, but, I promise you, the *affaire* would have ended with *me* in the Prison de la Santé.)

The ethics of French chambermaids vary visibly from hotel to hotel and from *arrondissement* to *arrondissement,* thus no rule of thumb to deal with them is possible. Yet, in their behalf, let it be said their disgust is real when they see a "rich" American fon-dling a cat, treating it to gourmet food, and issuing complicated protective instructions on its behalf. These women are mostly from the country; they love animals but secondly to human beings. When their families aren't poor, they're certainly frugal, and the prospect of a pet being treated better than a baby affronts them.

I see their point. I can make a clear case for Louis, and sometimes, when the chambermaid is intelligent and interested, I try to ex-plain what Louis means to me. They understand when I say the word "*seule.*" Away from their families, they are authorities on lone-liness. I try to tell them that my husband is often far from home, that, even when we travel, the nature of his assignments forces him to Copenhagen or Brussels, and that I am frequently alone in a strange hotel, in a strange city, knowing no one. Louis is my link to sanity; he is an old and dear friend, and I can go to bed early and read with him on the coverlet, guarding, loving, and loyal.

1.

Louis XIV…

2.

Louis at the Place Panthéon, Paris . . .

...and, of course, at the Place Vendôme.

4.

Louis studies a Gaugin sculpture.

Maybe I'm a nut, I always say, but with Louis the empty days are somehow less bleak.

"But why," one particularly obnoxious *femme de chambre* asked, "do you not have a mouse instead?"

"A mouse?" I repeated, I'm afraid, with horror.

"Yes, madame," she insisted. "I have a little white mouse to whom I tell all my secrets." She leaned closer, and her eyes were blazing pinpoints. "From one point of view, madame, I believe he is not a mouse at all, but the miller's son, bewitched."

Well, let me make it clear. I love Louis, but I do *not* think he is the miller's son, bewitched.

CHAPTER FIVE

The
Cats
of Paris

Whatever the chambermaids say, I feel at home in Paris because Parisians seem to have a natural affinity for cats. And there are millions of them, gutter, stray, and alley, known to the French as the *chat gouttière*. He manages to maintain his dignity and keep his head perilously above water under the most adverse conditions. If not having a legal domicile establishes vagrancy, he is a vagrant —but not *quite*.

On Rue Jules Chaplain there is a colony of these cats who chose to live in that honored sixth *arrondissement*, rather than the more elegant eighth, for a very specific reason: Dominique's. Dominique's is a Russian restaurant whose service entrance is on Rue Jules Chaplain. There, through the kitchen windows, the aromatic odors of beef Stroganoff and chicken Kiev attract cats from adjoining *quartiers* where boring domestic cuisine predominates. The goodnatured Russian chefs at Dominique's spend most of their time offering fresh sturgeon, blini, Stroganoff to any cat who is hungry.

The line of cats forms to the right. It is orderly and well behaved. Nobody pushes or shoves, nobody is rude, because there is enough for all. The cooks lean out of their windows urging the cats to eat. *"Mange, Gigi! Mange, Minette. Mange, Chouchou! Mange, Tovarichki!"*

Scraps of beef come flying through the door; bowls of sour cream are lowered through the window. The cats eat until they are so sated with abundance that they would prefer a glass of bicarbonate of soda to that last slice of smoked sturgeon.

Enviously, Louis watched this feline breadline from the window of *chambre* 25 at the Lutèce, but that was as close as he ever got. A Siamese is not a panty-waist, but a tussle with any of those hoodlums would have developed into a gang war. They are unemployed cats who've developed muscle; Louis is a soft pet of a cat. He is no match for either the Apache cats or those who work for a living.

The butcher cats, for instance, are fat and sleek from the trimmings of *tournedos*. The *table d'hôte* cats who are employed by restaurants jump on the customers' laps and seduce them into sharing their omelets and *crème renversée*. The concierge's cat sits on her window sill all day, checking on the goings and comings of the tenants with the same suspicion of the concierge herself. The zoos employ cats to keep the mice away from elephants, who *detest* them.

I even know a cat who works in a famous department store and snoozes in the folds of a ball gown when she has nothing else to do. Another cat friend is a night watchman in a dry goods shop and takes his siestas in a pile of reduced-for-clearance brassières. The café cats who were raised on the smells of cognac and pernod won't have a drink with you, but they will gladly share your *sandwich de jambon*, if you insist. Cats add an air of respectability to the most unlikely places. They can even make a house a *home*.

The reason for this great surge in cat employment is a four-letter word: *mice*. Paris' mouse problem can't be helped. It would be easier to remove the Eiffel Tower than those millions of tiny mammals who inhabit the beautiful seventeenth-century buildings and their mansard roofs. This is a secret, but the Louvre has its quota, the Panthéon too, and it wouldn't surprise me at all if Monsieur le Président Charles de Gaulle heard rustlings and squeakings in his bedroom at the Elysée Palace each night.

Unfortunate is the Parisian who has a mouse and doesn't have a cat. One of my friends, who wouldn't be found dead with a cat in his possession (he feels they cast reflections on his masculinity and that only a great Dane is a suitable pet for a mannish man), discovered that a mouse (*or* mice) was living with him. The telltale signs were there. His crackers were quickly disappearing; his Camembert and Brie (unrefrigerated, of course) were no longer safe, and his sleep was interrupted by a strange pitter-patter in his walls.

"Get a cat," advised his neighbors, but my friend ignored their advice and instead tried every mousetrap sold in the Galeries Lafayette's astounding collection. He even baited the traps with a cracker and Camembert, but the mice preferred finding their own rations in their own way, and continued to live their *dolce vita*.

There is a time in every Parisian's life when he *needs* a cat. So you either buy one, find one, or borrow one from your neighbor, a friend, or the grocery store.

My friend was too embarrassed to ask me to lend him Louis, so he borrowed Minette, a Maltese of uncertain origin, from the *charcuterie*. Minette was acclaimed the best mouser on the street, and the *charcutière* who gave her this testimonial knew what she was talking about. Any mouse or roach entering that *charcuterie* did a turn-about-face when confronted with Minette's businesslike paws and her pointed ears, sharp enough to hear a mouse forty meters away.

My friend accepted Minette merely as another mousetrap. He offered her no more affection than he would to a steel and wood contraption. He fed her, of course, and installed a box of sawdust for her use, but gave her nothing over and beyond his duty. Left alone, Minette sat on the kitchen window sill washing her ears or slept in the sun and just wasted her time, while the mice continued to gourmandise the supplies. There was no stroking for Minette, no kind word in appreciation of her beauty and capabilities. And Minette grieved, and refused to perform.

Then came the morning when he woke to find Minette on his shoulder, purring her love at him and kneading his flesh with her competent paws. At that moment he fell irrevocably in love with her, and told her so.

In return, within twenty seconds Minette pushed her way into a closet and came out with a rather fat mouse who was *chez soi* in a crate of books. "Bravo!" said my friend, and immediately applied for permanent custody of Minette.

Louis and I visit them quite often. Coming back from his house one day, I was walking along Faubourg St. Honoré with Louis on my shoulder. (He likes window-shopping as much as I do.) We had just done Lola Prusac and Peau de Porc when we passed an art gallery. The dealer, at first, looked at us through his glass door with astonishment and then, as though an electric lamp had ignited in his brain, opened his door and pleaded with us to enter. "A mouse," I suspected. "Poor man, with no cat of his own, has to ask one in off the street."

I was right. Inside, there certainly was no cat, but, leashed to a table leg, a little dog whose coat looked like dirty white marabou. There were also many Bonnards, a few Vuillards, a Severini, and one amazing sculpture in wood.

"Can you guess what it is?" the dealer asked imploringly.

"It's primitive; it's wood; it's life size. I'd say New Guinea, but I really know *nothing* about these things."

"You're right and you're wrong. It's *Tahiti*, and it's a *Gauguin!*"

I gasped at the wonder of seeing a Gauguin sculpture and such a large one at that.

"Would you like to perform an experiment with me?" The dealer looked at me like a frustrated Frenchman. "*So*," I thought, "*this is it*. At last I've been insulted!" I reached for my compact to blind him with Guerlain powder (one of your very best weapons) when he explained.

"Madame," he said, "there is something very peculiar about the Gauguin from the day it was shipped from Tahiti until the day it arrived here in Paris. Every dog who sees it runs *ventre à terre*[1] to get away from it. I must keep my own darling dog tied to the table leg to keep him from fleeing."

The art dealer (who shall be Monsieur D——) had been told that cats have an affinity for witchcraft, the mysterious, the unexplainable. He wanted to see what one would do when confronted with the Gauguin figure. I was shaking with anticipation. It was like one of Rod Serling's *Twilight Zones*.

We locked the gallery door, put the dog into the *lavabo*, and I removed Louis's leash to let him browse. He looked at the Bonnards, then spent a great deal of time in front of a Severini gouache (you see, he *knows* Severini). He wasted only a moment on a Vlaminck and then headed slowly for the Gauguin figure. Monsieur D——clutched my hand (a little *too* strongly, but I was compact-ready) as Louis began to inspect it with the air of a monocled art critic. He stepped away to see it better, then he sharpened his claws on the figure's thigh, yawned, and mewed to leave.

[1] Like a shot out of hell.

Monsieur was crestfallen. Now he was more bewildered than ever. What was it about the Gauguin that frightened dogs and not cats? Was there some mysterious spirit inside the figure that cast a spell upon dogs? I suggested he sell the figure, go into analysis, or consult a medium. He said indignantly, *"Madame s'amuse?"* And I had to admit that Madame was indeed herself amused.

Madame also solved the riddle, but he won't know unless he reads this. Months later, at a café in St. Tropez, I listened to the amazing adventures of a yacht captain who had formerly been a first mate on the Pacific run and had spent much time in Tahiti. Between his descriptions of the *belles poitrines* and the geographic splendors of that jewel of an island, I told him about the Gauguin wood sculpture and its mysterious effect on dogs.

"Chérie," he said, *too* like a Frenchman, "there is no mystery. That was wood from the koola-koola tree [or something like that]. It is, how you say, *aromatique, n'est-ce pas? Les* dogs hate it, because it smells of cats, but *les chats* like it—it just smells like themselves."

I told Louis, and he smiled. He knew all the time.

Cats *do* have a sense of humor. I can prove it. One summer a small rather shabby circus set up its weather-beaten tent at Porte de Vincennes. Its owner, desperate to steal customers from the Cirque Médrano, thought up an absolutely original act which he was sure would have us all in the aisles. The plan was to *train cats* to walk the tightropes, climb ladders, open doors, and stand on their hind legs to beg for a measly scrap of stale bread. He should have known better.

For this is by no means a simple achievement. Have you ever seen a cat act? Dogs, yes. But cats, pussy cats? Tigers, leopards, lions after great travail can be taught some tricks.[2] But pussy cats? I've never heard of it.

Yet this man was bound to do it. First, he had to find cats who would do anything at all for a saucer of milk. That was easy; it's not too hard to find four cats in Paris who are hungry enough to submit to a rigid training routine. "What the hell," they said, "when you're down and out, a job's a job." So they drank his milk and ate his meat and, when their reflexes were sufficiently conditioned, climbed his ladders, opened his doors, and walked his tight-

[2] Did you ever read Jack London's book on animal training? You'll never applaud a bicycling bear again.

rope. They rehearsed and rehearsed and swallowed their pride as they cringed under his rude insults and cruel whips. It was a miracle, the dress rehearsal. The cats behaved admirably.

But *"Le jour arrivera!"* was their motto, and the day did arrive —one Saturday night—and I was there.

The highly brushed and manicured cats sat patiently on the side lines waiting for their turn while a mangy monkey performed a silly dance with a tambourine. Their faces had deadpan expressions and they seemed to be so lifeless and lethargic that I felt they had been drugged. The monkey took his bows to a round of scattered applause and then a fanfare of trumpets and a roll of a drum announced the star attraction. *"Messieurs-dames,* for the first time in any ring, four *trained* cats, for your pleasure!"

At that moment, they were supposed to jump into the ring—boom! And jump they did—boom!—right off their bench, under a flap of the tent, and out into the night. Their boss was dumfounded and screamed terrible oaths at his disappearing actors, through the cheers of the audience. His unspeakable (and untranslatable) curses drifted into the *Gauloise*-smoke-filled air, unheard. The audience was too busy laughing.

Or perhaps they were thinking they'd like the cats' pelts for arthritis. You heard me. In France, a cat's skin is used to make a rheumatism mitt. Practically every drugstore in France has a window display of these macabre pelts waiting to be taken home by some poor arthritic who believes that the fur of a dead cat will cure him. I have news for those Frenchmen with bursitis in their joints —a warm, purring, live kitten, asleep on your knee, is far more efficacious!

Some people steal cats for food (rabbit is *not* always rabbit). Some people (I'm not mentioning names but they wear kimonos and eat rice) steal cats because nothing in the world makes a better *samisen* than a cat skin. Some people kidnap cats because they want the ransom. (This insidious blackmail is confined to the fancier breeds and I can just see these black villains searching the lost-and-found columns while their kidnaped victim, I hope, is doing all sorts of naughty things on their carpets.)

A child I know in Paris, the daughter of a famous painter, Arbit Blatas outwitted a pair of cat stealers all by herself. One day, when the family cat, Domino, didn't return for dinner, Dorothée conducted a street-to-street search for her errant darling. "Domino!"

she cried as she looked up into the chestnut trees. But Domino was not there. Neither was Domino sitting under the wall of the Santé prison, nor on the roof of the sculptor Auricost's studio.

Then two men in black came down the Boulevard Arago. One was carrying a burlap bag; its weight was considerable because he would stop once in a while to ease his shoulder. It was during one of these pauses that Dorothée heard a faint miaow. There was no doubt that it was Domino calling for help. There were other familiar miaows too. Dorothée, who understood cat talk, heard Kiki, Domino's aunt, and Chouchou, the concierge's Siamese, and the twin white Russian blues who lived, paradoxically, with one of the members of the French Communist Party. And Dorothée did not hesitate, but ran to the rescue.

She managed to reach the gruesome twosome just before they had the chance to dive into the Métro station. Standing at her full height of forty-eight inches, she pointed a finger at them and accused them of their black crime. They disputed her accusations and insisted the bag was filled with charcoal and firewood. Denials were useless against the wild screaming. No charcoal or firewood could writhe or make such excruciating noises. Dorothée shouted for the gendarmes, tripped the men, and, while kicking them with her heels, untangled the complicated sailor's knot which held the sack together.

Out they came, cat after cat, freed from the indignity of a death in a back-alley abattoir. Dorothée smiled triumphantly at her five friends. "If I hadn't come, you would have been sausages and mitts for rheumatism." Then she patted Domino apologetically. "Not *you*, Domino. You would have been a collar on a coat on the Champs Elysées."

The gendarmes made short shrift of the thieves; the neighborhood later presented Dorothée with a cake inscribed to her valor; the grateful republic sent her a certificate of merit, fully notarized.

I, of course, immediately invited Dorothée to my hotel room when I heard this heroic tale, and she and Domino and Louis and I celebrated. We had lemon squash and *mille-feuilles*. The cats were to be treated to saucers of cream and bits of medium-rare *entrecôte* from my expensive lunch at the Berkeley.

I am mortified to tell you that Louis and Domino disliked each other on sight, spat invective at each other, and finally squared off and fought three rounds, while Dorothée and I screamed like banshees.

I was asked to leave the hotel.

Oh well, it didn't matter. We were going south, anyway, to see the gypsies.

CHAPTER SIX

The
Provinces

If you leave Paris for the rest of France and have no first-hand knowledge of hotels (those that accept cats and those that won't) the only sensible thing to do is to take yourself to Thomas Cook & Son or American Express and go over your problem with one of the assistant managers.

Not that *we* ever did it. Oh no, not us! My husband and I had a neurosis about not doing anything touristy.[1] Catch *us* at Cook's? Not on your life. Not even when *Life* magazine asked us to do a pictorial essay on the gypsies in the southeastern part of France, and we were on our way to the Hotel de la Regina (which is not its name).

Had we gone to Cook's we could have avoided the Hotel de la Regina, described and highly recommended by a knowledgeable expatriate as "a pergola-topped Victorian structure with gingerbread porches, three proper meals a day, a trio swaying through Strauss waltzes at teatime, complete with a staff of competent *femmes de chambre* . . . children playing on the immaculate beach supervised by starched *gouvernantes* against a blue sea, seen from your balconied window, if the scarlet geraniums planted in blue faïence pots allow you to share it with them."

[1] *Not* doing anything touristy is an inverse snobbery of which I am guilty in the first degree. It means you never eat in the best restaurants, rarely see a rose window, and, above all, avoid the show at Le Lido.
Q. You know what I want to do most the next time I go to Paris?
A. See the show at the Lido.
Q. Why?
A. It has a trained cat.

Well, our knowledgeable expatriate was right—but in the wrong city. His Hotel de la Regina, it turned out, was in quite another town.

Our Hotel de la Regina was not Victorian, but fifteenth century. It had been tampered with by amateur bricklayers in the nineteenth century and apprentice carpenters in the twentieth, until its exterior resembled a Long Island roadhouse of the twenties with its eaves and towers outlined in purple neon tubing. Yet, statistically, it was the best hotel available in the region of La Camargue. It had to be; it was the only one. It was third class, the service unbearable, the plumbing installed by Charlemagne, and the food fit for pigs. And in April, it's a snake pit.

April brings the gypsies for their annual conclave, or peace conference, or nominating convention. They descend on this little village by every known means of conveyance: in stainless-steel caravans, horse-drawn wagons, delivery trucks, Cadillacs, Masseratis, and Maxwells. The poor gypsies (and there *is* a caste system) hitchhike, or walk—but on April 16 their meeting place has ten thousand *hommes* instead of four hundred. Why they pick on this town depends upon whom you ask.

The mayor says because it's in the center of France, which it is not.

The postmaster says a gypsy king loved a native girl who fell from a cliff, and the conclave is in her memory. A sad story but clearly apocryphal, because there are no cliffs.

Monsieur B——, the hotel owner, says because the village has the fewest gendarmes in France, and *that* I'm ready to believe.

Monsieur B—— does everything in his power to barricade his joint against the gypsies. They do not want rooms; they simply want to use the W.C. The side entrance to the hotel leads directly to the W.C., and one of the town's two gendarmes (Monsieur B——'s brother-in-law) does twenty-four-hour sentry duty at his post. Despite his vigilance, the gypsies manage to slip in, in a flash of golden earrings and a flutter of ruffles. As I sat in the lobby, I could feel their eyes on me. Not on me, really. On Louis.

The gypsies began to eye him as a good investment, especially those Teddy Boys in tweed coats with solid gold buttons, who spent hours on the terrace of the hotel drinking *pastis* and watching the girls go by. Not that the girls were anything to Bardolate; these chicks were uncorseted and unbrassièred, in ankle-length, gathered skirts, slimy beads around their necks, gold coins hanging from their wrists, and hoop earrings dangling under their unshampooed hair. They were uniformly dirty and half safe, but nonetheless the classic gypsy so mysteriously found in Canada, the U.S.A., the U.S.S.R., France, Italy, and Spain. Classic or not, they all looked at Louis with greed and craven longing. Did they want to cook him? Was "émincé of Siamese cat" a gypsy gourmet recipe? Or did they think I'd pay a handsome ransom for his return?

I had no intention of finding out, so Louis went wherever I did. I habitually wore a blue linen dress, short white gloves, and I carried a tightly furled umbrella, just in case. I let Louis perch on my shoulder, with his leash firmly held in my hand.

When they saw *that*, the gypsies smiled and bowed and scraped. I was puzzled until Monsieur B—— explained they thought I was a performer.

They bowed and stopped me on the street to ask the questions on their clever little minds. What was my act? They wanted to know. Did Louis tell fortunes like a parrot? Did he dance like a bear? Perhaps jump through a hoop? Did I plan to set up a tent and charge fifty francs for a sight of this rare beast from the jungles of Sumatra? And what *was* he? A mink? A marten? A sable? They obviously had never seen a Siamese and consequently put too high an opinion on Louis's value and rarity.

That worried me, so I asked Monsieur B——, who, by now, had become my liaison officer, to notify the king or the crown prince or whoever was in command of the conclave that Louis was only a Siamese cat, worth absolutely *nothing*. He was also to be told that Louis was fierce, scratched intruders, and would not hesitate at all to bite the nose of a child who came too close to him. Monsieur B—— delivered my white paper to His Majesty, who obviously put it high up on the agenda. So Louis was simply a cat! How they laughed! For, to a gypsy, a cat is an emblem of respectability—and they agreed he was worth absolutely nothing. Gypsies, whatever else they are, are not cat stealers.

But a cat lover, that is something a gypsy understands. An elderly lady gypsy stopped to pat Louis and spoke to him in Italian. She was surprised that Louis understood it, and more surprised that I did. (Mine is pure gutter Italian, picked up from butchers and tobacconists, so completely clear to gypsies.) She said she was a painter of Montenegrin ancestry, and discussed her passion for non-representational forms. I was surprised that she knew so much about modern painting, but I brushed away the thought that she knew where all the stolen Van Goghs in Europe were hidden.

I asked her to join me for a midmorning breakfast. We sat at a sidewalk café. She ordered mussels. I ordered corn flakes. Then she ordered corn flakes, too, and adored them. I knew I had her in my pocket.

I must have gypsy blood in me because this coffee break was a calculated risk. Up to now, my husband and I had managed to get only the most obvious photographs, the kind *anybody* could take with a Kodak. *We* wanted unique ones. And so I turned on all my charm, and Louis turned on his, and this delightful *tzigane* listened to my proposition.

For twenty-five hundred francs (old ones) and an expensive hair-brush, she agreed to take me to a session of the conclave, but secretly. Blue linen and white gloves were out. Would I dress as a gypsy and bring Louis? (Helps support us, Louis does.) Certainly I would. What should my husband wear?

"Oh no, signora, no husband."

So I, who cannot put a nail in the wall, was instructed in the deep mysteries of a Nikon by an extremely miserable and worried husband. Then together we got me up in faded blue jeans, did my hair with an egg beater, and applied black mascara to my toes. My husband, a genius at disguise, made an improvised necklace of a toilet chain, clipped three pairs of earrings together to make one— and, *voilà*, I was a gypsy! When I looked in the mirror, I frightened myself.

So, confidently, I joined my friend, swaggering like Marlene Dietrich, and marched down the main streets of the town en route to the conclave (my Nikon in an old evening bag) when a Jaguar screamed to a stop, and two English people jumped out. They were not Alec Guinness and Kay Walsh, but that'll give you an idea. From Nîmes, they'd come to see us gypsies—and would we permit a photograph?

My friend made the sign of the evil eye. I went her one better. I spit at them. *That's* when the shutter clicked and Alec announced jubilantly to Kay: "What a shot! A *real* gypsy and her cat. By jove, wait till they see this in Lewes!"

So, ladies and gentlemen, if you are ever in Lewes and see a photograph of a *real gypsy* and her *cat*—you'll be gypped!

I've dined out a good deal on my twenty minutes as a gypsy, proving that traveling with a cat through the *provinces* of France makes you a marvelous dinner partner.

I'm afraid my face gets red when I tell some of my other experiences: the time I stayed at a glorious hotel on the Riviera, for instance. I had a balcony with an unbelievable view of Cap Ferrat, Villefranche, even Corsica, in vibrant Raoul Dufy colors. Bougainvillea added its scarlet to the landscape and I noticed how cleverly it had been trained to climb over and below so that its abundance completely hid the balcony of the room next door. How discreet, I thought, the French were to make a beach balcony a private bower where lovers could have tête-à-tête breakfasts in *robes de chambre*. My neighbors, whose dim voices made it clear they were terribly and illicitly in love, were forever anonymous to everyone—to everyone, that is, but Louis.

It took more than bougainvillea to keep Louis where he belonged. A graceful leap over the flowery wall and, before I could scream *"No!"* he was exploring the contents of opened trunks, sniffing the bottles of Arpège, sipping the champagne, and thoroughly surprising Mademoiselle now in the convenience, to say nothing of Monsieur back in bed. Monsieur caught Louis by the tail, then opened his door and unceremoniously threw him out into the corridor, screaming wildly. Both of them.

I rushed to my door and caught the merest glimpse of Monsieur, who used to be a producer at what used to be a studio in Hollywood. While I was debating what to say to his wife, should I ever meet her, Louis, appalled at this manhandling, decided to escape.

Down the stairs he went, through the lobby, and the chase was on. It was complicated when I started after him, suddenly realizing I was wearing a transparent short nightgown. I rushed back to my room, found I had locked myself out, screamed for help, and was duly answered by screams from ladies below who *hated* angry Siamese.

Holding my hands where they did the most good, I proceeded to the lobby, on to the porch, snatched a tablecloth from one of the tables, used it as a toga, and proceeded to chase Louis through an alley into the casino, and caught him at last on a baccarat table.

Since I did not have a card of admission and the gendarmes were after me for indecent exposure, the only thing to do was sob, and leave town as rapidly as possible.

I learned two things from this experience:

1. Smile reassuringly when you meet an ex-producer and/or his wife.

2. *Never* take a hotel room with a balcony.

2a. Never take a hotel room on the top floor with a fireplace.

It may be that your cat will go out the chimney and down the next one, in which case you may meet an embarrassed Argentinian with a very charming young Japanese friend.

The Argentinian complained bitterly to the management. But, because I was quiet and seething with good manners, and the Argentinian was loud, threatening, and anti-cat, it was he who was thrown out. The Japanese young man turned up the next week with a new friend, and *they* sent me yellow roses.

Actually, only once were we refused a *chambre* in France because of Louis. It was in Mâcon, the gastronomical dead center of France. Nothing more luxurious than the thought of a comfortable room in Mâcon, a hot bath, and a divine dinner, with the regional wine. Louis, too, dreamed of some *foie de veau*, a sandbox, and a deep, wide chair in which to sleep. Unfortunately, a covey of wine merchants had descended upon Mâcon the day before we did and every hotel listed in the Guide Michelin, from the two-turreted *grand luxe* to the simpler (but excellent) establishments were SRO. Any hotel in Mâcon not listed in the Guide Michelin is not discussable, but where else were we to go? I no longer cared if roaches inhabited the bathrooms, if the sheets were not changed, or if the table linen was damp. Louis, my husband, and I wanted and needed a bedroom and a bathroom *at once*. A tiresome tour of the city brought us to a back street where we found a little hotel with blinking neon signs stretched across its sixteenth-century gables. I hesitatingly inquired if there was a *chambre avec salle de bain*. To my astonishment, there was not only *one* but five at my disposal. I was overjoyed and ran out to get my husband and cat. The receptionist found no objection to my husband—but Louis was quite another matter.

"*No animals! Absolutely no animals!*" The receptionist was livid. "*No beasts.* You *Americans* always travel with *beasts!* You are beasts! You ravage our land! You drink the blood of the workers. Out! You and your filthy capitalist cat!"

The hotel was probably Communist headquarters for the town

of Mâcon and obviously the receptionist was the local commissar. Louis and I now have excellent credentials should the House Un-American Activities Committee ever decide to call us as witnesses. Cats are a great help politically, too, you see.

CHAPTER SEVEN

Italy
and a
Prince

Once you cross the borders at Vintimiglia you leave your hotel troubles behind, as far as cats are concerned. With humans, it's different because Italian law covering hotels is chillingly specific, and varies from city to city only in the intensity of its enforcement. Bring all the dogs and cats you want upstairs but, come twilight, *never* a human being, no matter of what sex—that is, if you have a bedroom. If you have a suite, you may entertain at any hour, but watch out for the Italian equivalent of the man with the derby, the cigar, and the very flat feet.[1]

Most of the top Italian hotels are owned by one company—the Grand and Excelsior in Rome, for instance, and all the other Grands and Excelsiors in Milan, Genoa, Florence, and Naples. It's a lovely company with nothing but animal lovers on its board of directors.

Even the privately owned hotels, the Gritti and the Bauer-Gruenwald in Venice, and the Hassler in Rome, just *dote* on pets. It was a tossup whether the Hassler loved Audrey Hepburn more than her Yorkshire terrier. (It always astounds me when I see them together. They *look* alike.)

Only the Grand in Verona (apparently a maverick among all the other grand Grands) took exception to Louis. The reason we were in Vernona was to photograph Maria Callas at her earliest con-

[1] Siesta, one to four, is the time for entertaining your friends, whether old or new-found. Hearsay, of course.

venience (her latest convenience was almost three weeks). We informed her then husband of the hotel's intransigence, and he informed his wife, and his wife must have called the hotel, playing the full prima donna, because you never saw a hotel change its mind so thoroughly and so rapidly.

Same thing happened in Capri. We were doing some studies of the island and its natives, and couldn't get in to Gracie Fields's hotel. Miss Fields got us into a *pensione* downhill and, when they were shy of Louis, she read them the riot act in her sturdy Yorkshire Italian. It worked.

I'm sorry it did.

The *pensione* was built on an anthill.

A grain of sugar, a crumb, a pinch of Parmesan cheese dropped accidentally in your hotel room was enough to bring on an ant army which had obviously been waiting to open a second front. You can imagine the maneuvers when the generals heard about a full plate of Louis's lamb kidneys left unguarded in a corner of room 9.

Their advance lines were three inches wide; their rear guard, about two. Red ants, black ants, little ants, and larger ants; some with wings, some without—all arrived to eat Louis's lunch. Louis fought back; I screamed.

A piece of information I remembered from the Book of Knowledge, Volume III, emerged from the depths of my subconscious, heaven only knows by what process, and a little voice said: "Ants never cross water!" So I foiled the ants of Capri—perhaps the only woman alive who can make that statement. I filled a large platter with water, placed the kidney dish in the center, and waited for results. Slowly, slowly, the ants withdrew. Their confusion and frustration was a joy. But my victory was short-lived. They held a strategic meeting, regrouped, and, horrified, I watched ants' inhumanity to ants. The stronger ants killed the weaker and used their bodies to form a bridge. I defiantly put more water in the pan, and after an agonizing half hour the ants departed in defeat.[2]

I, of course, in my nicest manner, reported this incident to the manager. He immediately dispatched a maid to my room with a

[2] Having a nice lie-down with egg on your face (a damned good mask) can attract ants, too, especially if your bed is in a nice seaside resort like Ravenna Marina or Coney Island. Put each of the four legs of your bed in little bowls of water. *Ants never cross water:* Book of Knowledge, Volume III.

large spray can of official American army DDT. Most Europeans believe that DDT can kill anything. It can, even cats. Watch them aim that spray gun filled with the deadly mist on anything in the room as though they were perfuming the air with Chanel No. 5. It's a killer, that DDT, and whether it settles in your nose or on a cat's dinner, it can't possibly do as much good as it does harm.

There are other poisons, obviously, too. Look carefully in almost any bathroom in Europe, and you'll see a trail of yellow powder outlining the floor, around the tub, toilet, basin, and bidet. Oh, the color is divine. I had a suit done in it, poison yellow. Did I say poison? That's what it is—poison for roaches, you, and your cat! It's arsenic, pure sweet arsenic! Only thing to do is to borrow a broom, sweep it up, and mop the floor afterward with good strong soap and hot water. If you don't, the first lick a tidy cat takes in washing it out of his hair may be his last.

Or a fly may do him in, in the end. You never see screens in French or Italian hotels. You can keep a cat *in* by pulling the shutters closed but you can't keep the flies *out*. And once they enter, they multiply into a vast population explosion.

Madame Mouche arrives late one afternoon and decides to lay her eggs on your cat's dinner or your soufflé. Then her sisters and her cousins and her aunts join the fun and turn your hall bedroom into a maternity ward. In a few hours their little blessings hatch into small white specks that vaguely resemble grains of farina but are *most* definitely *not*. These, my friends, are larvae, which quickly change into that next stage of fly growth, the maggot (one of nature's more repulsive sights). Flies grow from egg to adult in public or private. I didn't know this until Louis told me the facts of a fly's life. Not really *told* me. We understand each other by telepathy. He turned up his nose at his dinner, after examining it carefully.

"Take that plate away," he was trying to say. "Can't you see it's tainted? Ugh! That sprinkling of little white things is *not* Parmesan cheese, or didn't you ever hear about flyspecks?"[3]

Then I organize a ruthless Murder Inc. in fly season. First a fly swatter. If that doesn't work, a Rube Goldberg invention of attaching ribbon streamers to an electric fan. (You can always find one in Europe.) Whatever I do, I *don't* use fly spray. The label may

---

[3] A cat who eats these specks develops into an incubator for W-O-R-M-S. For further information, see your veterinary.

assure me that it contains no DDT, but would *you* like your veal *Piccata* flavored with it?

All these insecticides are part of a massive Italian effort to deal with an overabundance of flies, mosquitoes, hornets, ants, and a mixed bag of flying and crawling things. In the end, to accomplish this, the Italians will have to drain the swamps and clean the cesspools—eventually undergo a gigantic urban renewal.

But while the Bureau of Sanitation is working out a master plan against the insects, it is doing nothing whatever to control the cat population.

In the Mussolini era and during the German occupation, the Italians lost most of their cats. They starved; they were eaten; they fled. But cats, while they do not have quite the vital statistics of rabbits, manage to procreate rapidly. The gestation period for a cat's pregnancy is sixty-eight days; a female can have a litter of as many as six kittens; the same female can have upwards of twenty litters in a lifetime.

And in Rome the whole process appears to be in double time. There are more cats than Romans, and that is not a happy statistic. The Romans say jovially, "A cat in every home," as we used to say, "A car in every garage." Well, if you divide the cats of Rome up equally, each home would have at least five.

Only they don't. Most of the cats are strays and apparently they've become a tourist attraction.

A schoolteacher friend of mine, touring Rome in a Cook's charabanc, told me that the tourist buses stop at the Forum, the Pantheon, the Coliseum, and the Largo Argentina, to display the darling cats of Rome. I could hardly believe it, so I took one of the tours. Now I believe it. It's a sickening sight.

In the Largo Argentina, the site of four temples, now excavated below street level, a veritable cat nation exists. There may be four thousand cats, or perhaps four hundred thousand. Nobody knows, because it's impossible to take a census.

The life of a Roman cat, domiciled in a ruin, is short and not even sweet. The unprincipled ones survive; the ethical ones die young, even before they lose their baby teeth. The rules of the game are spartan: women and children *last*. No holds barred. Hate your neighbor. Eat him if necessary. *Survive, survive, survive!*

Oh, each colony has a leader—a president, or dictator, or Big Brother. There are first-, second-, and third-class citizens. There are ward heelers, Gestapo agents, Caspar Milquetoasts (they don't last long), and Paladins. Each spring a bumper crop of kittens arrives through incestuous love (everyone is related). Then nature's balance disposes of this population explosion. Exposure, disease, and malnutrition finish off most of the newly born, and if that doesn't do it, there are always the jaws of their elders. They die in droves; but more and more and more are born.

It's curious how. There is, in effect, a maternity ward which female cats use for their secret *accouchements*.[4] A pregnant cat, I assure you, will walk miles to reach this remote *soi-disant* lying-in hospital because it is insulated against the males. A high wall and several muscular neutered toms, who act as eunuchs, protect the *enceinte* mothers and their newborn from intruders with a battering ram of spits, hisses, and claws—male intruders, that is, with cannibalism on their filthy little minds.

Birth control societies, spurred on by veterinaries, are trying their best to convince Romans that sterilization is the best thing that could happen to their cats. But who can convince these Latins (who are *not* lousy lovers[5]) that castration is not an outrageous crime? A *castrato* (neutered) male is pitied, his owner condemned.

I have a cat so pitied; I am an owner so condemned.

Yes, Louis is *castrato*. (But I assure you he cuts a beautiful figure of a male, and in his time has dazzled more than a few dandy females. He has also left them frustrated.)

I was awarded the Scarlet Letter on the terrace of the Cafe Rosatti, in Piazza del Popolo. Louis was sitting in his usual chair, looking handsomer than ever. An even handsomer gentleman to our right kept staring. I shifted and reached for my umbrella.

When he rose and came toward us, my heart fluttered.

"I am Prince T——," he said.

"I am Beulah Roth," I said.

"I dislike to intrude," he said.

"What may I do for you?" I asked.

"It is a delicate matter." He hesitated, then he looked at the fourth finger of my left hand and saw the wedding ring. "Signora . . ."

---

[4] I don't want the Board of Health to swoop down, so I think I'd better not reveal the exact location. Believe me, it does exist because I saw it, and I've never been quite the same.
[5] Hearsay, of course.

"Not too delicate, I hope," I said archly, and then I added, "Prince."

"Signora," he said, clearing his throat, "it is a question of romance, to use a euphemism."

My husband was due to meet me in ten minutes. I hoped—oh, how I hoped—he wouldn't be early. Not that I planned an assignation with the Prince—but there's something about an Italian in a handmade suit from Battistoni, the faint smell of Sen-Sen, and a euphemism, that are irresistible temptations to try to be young again.

"Romance?" I said in a cracked voice. "I'm not quite sure I know what you mean." I knew very well what he meant.

"My wife and I, signora," said the Prince—and *that* stopped me —"have a superb Siamese cat—a female—who up until this point has rejected all suitors."

"What a pity," I said, and what a pity, I thought.

"You have," continued the Prince, "a superb example of the species. I should like . . ." He hesitated again. "I should like to suggest a liaison."

"I'm afraid that's quite impossible, Prince," I said miserably.

"Oh," he said, "not a sordid liaison. I am suggesting marriage."

I hesitated, lit a cigarette to cover my panic, waited another moment, and then said in a very small voice, "*Signor il principe,* I regret more than I can tell you that my cat is—how shall I put it? —*castrato.*"

He drew himself up and made a horrible little sniffing sound. Louis growled.

"*You* regret?" he said coldly. "It is the *cat* who regrets."

He did a military about-face and disappeared into the Piazza del Popolo.

I looked at Louis and wondered. To lose an opportunity like this to marry into the royal family? Not ever to have known romance? Not ever to have felt passion? Oh, Louis, what have I done to you?

Recklessly, I called for the waiter and ordered a lobster tail. When it was brought and I saw Louis eat it with such loving relish, occasionally looking at me adoringly, I knew, deep in my guilty heart, that there were things in life more satisfying than sex. . . .

For a cat, that is.

CHAPTER EIGHT

The
Via di Villa Ruffo

When Louis received this proposal we had already been in Rome for six weeks waiting for a film to start. The American company producing it in conjunction with an Italian company had contracted for my husband's services. But owing to a miserable combination of weather, temperament, and sniffles, principal photography had not begun. Massive sets had been built in Cinecittà; great galleys were floating in the Mediterranean; extras by the thousands were already engaged and costumed; still there was no starting date.

We chafed under this enforced idleness, debated whether to leave or to stay. My husband was constantly being assured that production would roll any day. We held a council of war and decided that, even if it did, it would take months to produce—and we were heartily sick of hotels and restaurants. And Louis was the sickest of all.

No, the picture was not *Cleopatra*. I won't tell you its name (because it was such a resounding bomb) but it was more than seven years before *Cleopatra*. Whenever I hear about runaway pictures and the money you can save by making pictures abroad, I laugh merrily. Were I a producer, I would never make a picture anywhere but in Hollywood where I could control the cast.

I well know from personal experience the boredom and insecurity of waiting around Rome for a picture to start—and what that can do to a husband and wife and a cat stuck in one hotel room week after week. That was why my husband and I held that famous council of war, after we found ourselves spending all our waking hours bickering. A marriage can survive screaming, shouting, and hysterics; it's doomed with the bickers. And my husband and I decided to do something about it.

We had one of two choices: to walk out on the picture contract or to take an apartment where we would not be constantly in each other's way. (Love flies out of the window of a double hotel room with cat after six weeks.) We tried the first course, but were threatened by Italian lawyers and cables from Hollywood. So we obviously had no choice but to try the second.

To find an apartment in Rome, with a cat, is not an easy business. Oh, there are those very stylish, modernistic new apartments at Parioli—but they're expensive, far from public transportation and shops, and like prison cells. They're also very touristy. What we wanted was an apartment with character. And we set our friends looking.

Anna Magnani is the best real estate agent in Rome; she knows everybody, and she drives a hard bargain. Through a friend of hers we discovered an ideal flat on the Via di Villa Ruffo. It was on a street that had only the Viterbo Station, then two apartment houses (ours was one of them), then Prince Ruffo's villa, then the annex of the French Academy. Opposite, there was only one building, which held the archives of the Department of Agriculture, and the Borghese Gardens. It was ideal, notwithstanding that, from an American point of view, it was on the wrong side of the tracks.

Even though it had extreme water problems (water was rationed for *all* purposes) and we had to walk up two flights, we took it because it was opposite the Borghese, and I could walk Louis through the near part of the park, which was, I'm afraid, severely neglected. Once there had been well-attended glens, glades, fountains, and serpentine walks. Now they were overgrown with weeds and nettles. Most of the pines, the celebrated pines of Rome, were dead or dying.

After we were settled in the flat (not exactly like moving into the Waldorf Towers), I walked with Louis daily through the exotic Arcadia of the Borghese, with my eyes focused on the ground under me, never knowing on *whom* or *what* I would step. Sometimes it was a sleeping man, sometimes a couple. There were broken bottles and mysterious packages nicely gift-wrapped, covered with ants. These contained garbage placed discreetly behind a bush by some genteel housekeeper who could not wait a week for the scavenger to

THE VIA DI VILLA RUFFO

collect it. After a few weeks, neither could I, and I wrapped my own garbage in shoeboxes from Ferragamo's (the only place in Rome that has shoes to fit me) and dropped it behind an obscure tree.

Once production started, my husband would bring people from the set home to dine—and cooking became as big a problem as the garbage. I slaved, and at the going Roman price for help, I was determined to find a maid. So I went to Anna Magnani again. She referred me to her domestic agency, and through them, there appeared in our lives the incredible Madellena.

Although her references were vague she proved to be a female St. Francis of Assisi, Cordon Bleu cook, passionate mopper, sweeper, turner of mattresses, superstitious fool, and devoted friend. Unlike the chambermaids of Paris, she needed no defense of Louis. She loved him on sight, and he loved her straight back. She had no royal blood, but Louis made a morganatic platonic marriage. I confess I was a little jealous.

Whenever I walked through the Borghese with Louis, Madellena would watch me from our sitting-room window, leaning on a pillow. We had a prearranged signal. When Madellena shrieked, "Madame!" I had no other choice but to flee the garden with Louis in my arms and head directly for the safety of our entrance hall across the street. There I would barricade myself behind the heavy wooden doors until the danger had passed. The "danger" was not a half-crazed heroin addict with a switch blade bent on murder, but another Siamese cat with the same intent. This fiend, who lived in the French Academy with a *portiera*, hated Louis and swore a blood feud. Madellena called him Stupido, only because, in her book, any cat compared to Luigi[1] had to be *stupido*. He wasn't. He had the brain of a Machiavelli, and a compulsive determination to make contact with Louis-Luigi, to throw a glove in his face and demand satisfaction with claws at dawn.

Hard as I tried to prevent this battle royal, it took place one day while I was having my hair done. The gas inspector arrived to check the meter and, as Madellena opened the door, Louis-Luigi escaped, ran down the flight of steps into Via di Villa Ruffo, then over the wall into the Borghese. Madellena and the gas inspector followed, but it was too late. Stupido was already on his way. The rest of the

[1] Madellena named Louis "Luigi Brontolone." *Brontolone* is the Italian noun for grumbler.

story I heard through Madellena's gasps as I washed her wounds with an antiseptic.

In a corner, Luigi was licking his. She swore, *mamma mia,* as Luigi's second, that it was a glorious fight. Louis, lighter and less accustomed to fighting, had turned into Jack Dempsey and Stupido had crawled away in utter defeat. Madellena and I celebrated with *vino*—and Madellena ran to the butcher to get Louis-Luigi an especially appetizing bit of spleen.

It was remarkable that she did, because Madellena hated the *tripier* with a terrible hatred for reasons unknown. I rather liked him myself. He was short and bald, had five gold teeth, mongoloid features, and a very gallant manner when dealing with ladies. Whenever I went to his stall in the open market on the Via Flaminia, he bowed and scraped and not only gave me the best of everything but *cut* it for me too. And in Italy that's extraordinary. What is even more extraordinary is that he would wrap it—using a clean sheet of newspaper for the purpose. And when I left, he would blow me a kiss with a baritone "A *domani.*"

The feud between Madellena and the butcher came to a head one day when the convenience in Madellena's bathroom overflowed. While this may not seem to be a *sequitur,* I assure you it is. A plumber, after hours of research, found, to my horror and amazement, that newspapers had been flushed down the you-know-what in such an abundance that the well-worn Roman sewage system had backed up.

"*Madellena!*" I lost my temper. "Why, oh, why did you have to use newspaper? I know you use the toilet as a garbage disposal, but then everyone does that for *little* things. Newspaper is inexcusable!"

Madellena said nothing to me until the plumber had left. "Madame," she then said indignantly, "it's *not* what you think. I did it for *you.* You know the *tripier* who sells you Louis's *milza* and liver?"

I nodded, knowing he'd get in the act.

"Well," said Madellena, "he is a Communist. Not only is *he* a Communist, but he wraps everything you buy in *Unita.*[2] Now, madame, think what could happen to you *if* the scavenger who takes our rubbish every day found those papers. Your *reputation,* madame! I was destroying the evidence!"

[2] Communist Party newspaper.

I changed *tripiers* for Madellena's sake, but a few months later the sewer backed up again—this time because of *Messaggero!*[3]

Madellena's politics were straight down the middle of the road. And my husband and I were headed straight down the middle of the same road to the loony bin, because at this point the picture was suspended because of more temperament and more bad weather.

So we decided to go to Spain for a holiday—with a stop-off in Madrid to see—can you believe it?—the bullfights.

[3] A conservative anti-Communist newspaper.

CHAPTER NINE

Olé!

I felt the ectoplasmic eyes of Aunt Jean on me from the moment I crossed the French border into Spain. For you who were *not* brought up in Brooklyn before and after World War I, I must explain Aunt Jean. She was nobody's aunt. In fact, she may have been an amalgam of many reporters, but her column in the Brooklyn *Daily Eagle* gave Brooklyn children of the era a consciousness about cruelty to animals. You joined her club—the Aunt Jean Humane Club—and vowed forever and ever and ever to be kind to dumb beasts. You learned how not to tie cans to dogs' tails; how not to paint a white streak down the back of a cat to have a skunk. I signed a statement for Aunt Jean once, promising never to wear feathers unless they were molted. I almost committed perjury by being tempted by a dress at De Barentzen's. The entire skirt was made of steely gray ostrich feathers, and anyone knows how it *hurts* the ostrich to have them pulled out. No, Aunt Jean won again; I remained *true blue*.

I've had some rather peculiar fellow club members. Recently in the London Zoo, on a cold Sunday morning, a lady in a mink coat was busily distributing largess from a market basket in the zebra and deer house. I followed her as closely as I dared without seeming presumptuous. (One has to be careful of this in London.) My curiosity overpowered me and I made up my mind to find out what she had in that basket. I tried sniffing but all I could get was a strong whiff of Diorissimo. Then I tried snooping and what I saw astounded me. The lady in the mink coat turned around and spoke to me. "Poor darlings," said she, "they just really never get any of the goodies from Fortnum's unless I bring them!"

The zebras and the antelope, to judge by their grunting, chomping, and chop licking, were no doubt appreciative of her gifts. There was Fortnum and Mason's own brand of imported spaghetti, intended to be served at those chic little after-theater suppers. Malaga raisins at 10/6 a pound, and those exquisite little chocolate peppermints and glacé fruits which Caprice serves with coffee.

"Watch them, darling! Just watch them! Isn't it marvelous?"

I watched and wondered how this seemingly outlandish food could give these fodder eaters so much pleasure. How had she come to the conclusion that *this* was what they liked? Her answer to my question was no surprise. "Trial and error, darling, just trial and error! I *love* animals. I cannot bear to see them harmed or hurt! Simply cannot *bear* it!"

"Of course," I said, "I feel the same way."

"I've pledged myself to care for all of them," she went on, "and to *slave* to prevent their destruction. I wouldn't *dream* of wearing feathers. Not dream of it!"

I could stand it no longer. "But what about your coat?" I asked.

"Coat?"

"Yes, coat; it's mink."

"Certainly it's mink, darling. I adore it."

"Well, mink's fur," I insisted.

She put her hands to her ears. "Don't tell me," she said, "I don't want to hear about it."

And off she went.

Well, in Spain, I couldn't live in *her* kind of dream world. I *had* to go and see the bullfights. And you want to know what happened to me?

I threw up.

I went back to the hotel, hugged Louis, and dreamed of Aunt Jean in Madrid at a bullfight, brandishing her umbrella at the matador and making her kill by sinking it between the torero's shoulder blades. "Olé!" I cried in fantasy. "Let us have no more of that! Down with the national sport of Spain!"

I *hate* bullfights, and all you aficionados who worship Hemingway and Barnaby Conrad can just get up and leave right now. I hate you too.

I was terrified, wondering what the Spanish did to cats. No need for terror. There are no cats. I may not have searched properly, but I counted only three: *Uno,* in a taxidermist shop, stuffed, of course!

Dos, ditto dead, decomposing on a beach. And on the third one hangs a tale of the town of Zarauz.

The Gran Hotel at Zaruaz is *the* grand hotel. It overlooks the sea and a rather unpleasant dark, murky, gray sea it is, too, with fierce breakers, roaring toward the beach. No castanets clackety-clack, nor do flamencos amuse the guests, for the Gran Hotel is most properly British. Plaster and beam exterior, primroses and wallflowers in the garden, chintz on anything that bears covering. Even the food, served by starched waitresses, who just *had* to be trained in some Eaton Square scullery, had that lackluster, insipid quality for which provincial British hotels are noted.

In spite of the fact that American tourists vacationing in Spain found the atmosphere odd, the British enjoyed every moment. Like snails, carrying their homes on their backs, they were not separated for a moment from their morning kipper, their London *Times,* their Earl Grey tea, their well-done joint, or their custard sauces. Even the sheep who grazed in those Basque hills began to grow accustomed to the "darlings" which echoed through the valleys, and the Bentleys and Jaguars whizzing through their erstwhile pastoral solitude.

I never forgot that I was in Spain, even though Fortnum and Mason permeated the air. Louis was closely guarded all through the day and night. The door to our room was locked securely and the key in my bodice in the style of Theda Bara. You can imagine my astonishment, one day at tea, when a very gentle lady with a Knightsbridge accent informed me quite casually that Louis looked amazingly well when she saw him sitting on a bicycle in the village.

"Are you sure it was *Louis?*" I asked.

"Of course, my dear. He is *Siamese,* isn't he?"

Indeed he is Siamese! Indeed, on a bicycle! Next thing will be that Louis performed a veronica in the bull ring! Hallucinations?

The news of Louis's exploits began to drift to me throughout tea and dinner. Someone had seen him on the road to Pamplona, another on a fishing boat going out to sea, still others nibbling an octopus in the market place, or in the arms of the local *fille de joie.* Impossible? Maybe not!

Of course it was *not* Louis. I knew that Louis was asleep on the Jacobean chintz chair when he was observed in town. Was it a mirage? Or was there another Siamese cat in Zarauz? One assumption was as questionable as the other, but I was more inclined to distrust shadow than substance. So there I went again, Louis on my shoulder, securely attached to me by claw and lead, into the town. If there were another cat I'd soon know; if there were *not* —a supposition too dismal to think about—Louis was definitely a witch's cat and I was the *witch!*

For the first time, the tables were turned. Louis was mistaken for that *other* one. First it was the fishwife who asked Louis why he hadn't come for his octopus. The *fille de joie*, attempting to stroke Louis's back (with an expert's hand), received a bloody rebuke. "What's the matter with you today? Don't you know me?"

Through the streets we walked. Louis returned each greeting, "*Día,*" with a hiss and a snarl. He showed disapproval to the entire population of Zarauz, who, being un-Spanish, as Basques claim to be, genuinely liked cats.

When you want to know about cats—ask the butcher. But he asked *me!* "What are you doing with *my cat?*"

Before I could answer, *his* cat made an entry, timed perfectly to fit the crisis. It certainly was a Siamese—but there the similarity stopped. If any of the gossipmongers had taken the time to lift this cat's tail, they would have known at once that it was not a señor, but a señora.

So, laughing again, we went back to Rome. The director, at long last, was again screaming, "Speed! Camera! Action!"

CHAPTER TEN

A
Letter
to a Friend

As the months wore on, the movie absolutely refused to be finished. I was perishing of boredom and ennui. I had shopped; I'd been to every picture gallery and I'd seen every ruin; I'd read every English book and magazine in Rome; I was beside myself with uselessness. So I tried to write a novel, an occupation for which, I found almost immediately, I had no talent.

And then one day I got a letter from Los Angeles from a friend of mine who had just bought a brace of Siamese cats. She asked me what to feed them, how to bring them up, and what to do if she should ever take them to Europe. And I wrote her a series of letters that was sort of a little textbook.

Let's face it. You're about to see how this whole shmear began!

DEAR PEG:

I cannot tell you how delighted I am to hear that you and Paul have gotten yourselves two Siamese cats. I'm delighted with their names: Kubla and Khan—nice and oriental and sinister, but very appropriate. Not that it really matters *what* you call them. I discovered long ago that a cat doesn't ever know its name. It's the sound of your voice that he obeys. And don't expect too much obeying either.

But do expect a lot of cheer, and fun, and exasperation. But the first warning I must give you is never to close a closet door without looking carefully; Siamese have a curious way of slinking by you into the dimmest recesses of your linen closet. If you close it, you'll spend the entire day fretting, and swearing they've been stolen.

When they come out they'll be hungry. They're always hungry— except when they refuse to eat. Refusal to eat is not necessarily a sign of indigestion; it may be a sign of moral indignation. Siamese cats are insulted very easily, and they're very picky about their food. So keep your larder well stocked.

If you don't, there'll come the black moment in your life when you'll discover there's nothing for your cats to eat in the cupboard, refrigerator, freezer, or garbage can. That's what *always* happens to me.

I never seem to learn my lesson. Putting things away for a rainy day, keeping a supply of fresh water in case of attack, or buying a carton of cigarettes instead of a package is not in my blood. Sometimes I forget that Louis is a cat and that I cannot send him to the corner grocery store for a half pound of liver. It isn't so bad at home with supermarkets open for twenty-four hours a day, almost at your front door. But when a Frenchman or an Italian or, for that matter, a Spaniard leaves his shop for the day, woe to the housekeeper who has forgotten her *entrecôte.*

Once or twice, even though I *did* try, I arrived at the butcher's just in time to see the curtain clang shut over the entrance. No use banging at the door; no use pleading for just one little *tournedos;* no use offering a diamond ring in exchange for a sliver of heart—or yourself for a kidney. He's gone!

What do you do? You look up the street for some sign of life. There is the bakery with nothing but *madeleines* or *Sacher torten.* The *pasta-pane's* curtain is still up but nothing for a cat to eat, except possibly the baker himself. The greengrocer? Leeks and potatoes make a mighty good soup but not for a cat.

So you go back to your cozy little hotel room and begin a systematic search of the premises. You look among your lingerie for a forgotten can of cat food. You drag duffelbags and hand trunks from under beds, hoping to discover an unused sausage or a pastrami sandwich. You find some strange things—five hundred francs you had forgotten—a scarf thought stolen—two pairs of new nylons, *and* a lot of dust. Nothing for a cat!

Now there is only one thing left to do. Hungry or not, you go to Howard Johnson's or its continental equivalent, and order one hamburger (called mostly hamburger now everywhere but sometimes it's better to say "ground meat") *rare*, no mustard, no ketchup, no onions, and no bread! Or to a restaurant or bistro. Look at the menu for appearances' sake, choose something your cat likes, eat a portion of it, and demand that the leftovers be wrapped to take home to your cat.

Did I ever tell you about the timid little man, a civil servant, no doubt, who shared a table with us for many months at a small bistro in Paris, Le Corbeille, I think it was, on Rue Delambre? He never finished what was on his plate. When he demanded his *addition*, he pointed to his half-eaten *escalope* or *chateaubriand*, mumbling something about "*quelque chose pour le chat*," withdrew a legal-size envelope from his vest pocket, and deposited the remains of his dinner in it. What happened to it once he left the restaurant is your guess as well as mine. (Tomorrow's lunch was what I made out of it.)

I've never known a restaurant in Italy or France that wasn't co-operative when politely asked for "*quelque chose pour le chat*." What you receive is *not* always your own. Sometimes that *entrecôte* you judiciously refrained from eating is augmented by an assortment of chop bones, crusts of bread, fat trimmings, and gravy-soaked water cress, a mess that would look much better in a garbage can than in a cat's stomach. But sort it out, and the kids will have a nice lunch.

American restaurants ask no questions about the final destination of your leftovers. Say the magic word "cat" and immediately your half-empty plate is removed to the kitchen where the contents are deposited in a wax-paper-lined "Bowser" bag bearing the indecent inscription "For Fido."

Restaurant food, whether it comes from Barney's Beanery or Maxim's, must be rinsed free of all condiments, seasonings, and sauces before your cat can enjoy his secondhand supper. Ketchup, tabasco, mustard, paprika, Escoffier, and horse-radish don't have the same fascination for cats as they do for humans.

Dinner parties become another marvelous source of cat food. But whenever I am invited to one of those buffet dos, I always manage to be sure to share a table with people who have no animals. You can't imagine the squabbling that goes on when the plates are about to be removed if your dinner partners happen to have a carnivorous quadruped as a pet. You find yourself doing the Alphonse-Gaston routine with the gentleman at your left.

"Take the roast beef for your dog," you say.

"Oh no," he answers. "You take it for your cat."

He says it, but he doesn't mean it. He sneaks the leftover roast beef from his plate and yours into his napkin—and you're left with nothing, unless you happen to know the cook. Even if you know the cook, you discover that he has made arrangements for those leftovers too.

I won't tell you his name, Peg, because if there's anything I detest, it's gossip, but he's a director who's just made the absolutely worst picture in the world. I'm sure you'll be able to figure it out, so don't sit next to *him* at a buffet dinner.

Anyway, cocktail parties are better. Not that I'm too stingy to buy Louis his own shrimp and martinis, but the waste after the first hour and a half is so enormous that my hostess never knows the difference. A nice big handbag, which Gucci does for me in velvet (I'll get you one), with a wad of paper tissues for wrapping, serves me beautifully as a market basket. Sometimes people who don't know I have a cat and observe me pilfering the trays are falsely led to assume that I am a starving bohemian on the prowl for sustenance. The trouble is, Louis is very picky about what I bring home.

Theoretically, veterinarians seem to agree that a cat will eat anything *you* want him to eat, but I'm here to tell you, theory or not, the going is tough once a food pattern has been established. Actually, *nothing is too good for a cat,* but even I get impatient with statements like: "Mine won't touch a thing but kidney," or "Mine won't eat anything but shrimp," or "*Lulu* sniffs at anything but a filet mignon." A cat with a monkey on his back who has to have a *fix* of two-dollar-a-pound beef is a pretty expensive liability.

Once a bad eating habit has been established it takes great fortitude on the part of an owner to sit by and watch hour after hour go by with no sign of a cat relenting. Don't *you* relent either! The stubbornness of cats is often weaker than their stomachs. Even addicts of one and *only* one particular food are sometimes caught with their principles down and give in.

Some cats feel they are losing face if *they* eat what *you* want them to eat, and fight a cold war until you surrender and start deveining shrimp all over again. Surprisingly, other cats love the new *table d'hôte* and thank St. Gertrude that at last you've realized your cooking is a bore and you're changing the menu. *It takes two to tango!*

Well, darling Peg, Sandy just called from the studio and I've got to go out and meet him, and then we're going to dinner at La Fontanella. I'll get you those delicious tassels you want tomorrow, and I'll watch out for a decent pair of candlesticks at Porta Portese (more fake Renaissance junk there, these days, than real) and I'm furious that I can't see any of Paul's television shows here.

I'll write you again soon and continue with this cat business.

All my love,
BEULAH

P.S. I've just reread this letter and you know something, Peg? I really think I *am* crazy.

CHAPTER ELEVEN

Another
Letter
to a Friend

DEAR PEG:

I was supposed to go and have my hair done at a divine new place on Via della Vita, but it's been raining like stink for the fourth day in succession, and Madellena is in a foul mood because I discovered her putting newspapers down the toilet again. You see, it doesn't really matter whether it's *Unita* or *Messaggero;* Madellena is just too neat, and she'll never learn that the toilet isn't a trash basket.

I'm huddled in a sweater, because it's so cold, and the heating arrangement we have gives only luke warmth. The Borghese Gardens across the street are dismal and I long so terribly for the blue skies of California I can hardly bear it. The only time to be an expatriate is in the spring and summer; if I ever see Swall Drive again, I may never leave.

So do you mind if I write you again and go on with the business of cat foods? You really don't have to pay any attention to it; for me it's kind of solo therapy.

I've been thinking that I not only love Louis; I respect him. That's why we have such a good relationship. And if you respect a cat, you must respect his tastes, within reason. Some cats dote on fish, others hate it. Some drink a half pint of milk a day, some not a cupful in a lifetime. Crab meat, that highly publicized delight, interests Louis less than a piece of raw dough. Researching one's cat's likes and dislikes need not be a Herculean task. Just takes patience.

As a rule of thumb, you're safe with all proteins, meat and fish. But there is a little of the vegetarian in all of them. Lions, jaguars, tigers, and leopards don't take the time to sort out vegetable matter from flesh before sitting down to a late lunch in the jungle. The organs of their prey invariably contain leaves, grasses, fodder, fruits, and vegetables, and I can't imagine a hungry tiger refusing breast of zebra because he doesn't like spinach or eucalyptus leaves. The big cats, therefore, are not carnivores, but omnivores, as we are. (Dietetically, that means double-gaited.)

Still, the domestic cat has lived too closely to man not to have taken on some of his habits. (According to my dentist, cats are now developing caries because of soft foods.) But a cat is not a food faddist. He will resist all the new health food jazz: wheat germ, potassium broths, and blackstrap molasses! (Maybe Dr. Gayelord Hauser will have something to say about *that!*)

Nor is a cat a gourmet. He is not amused by Chateauneuf du Pape 1947. (He detests alcohol.) Truffles do not tempt him, nor do chocolate soufflés. He does very nicely without strawberries Romanoff, Caesar salads, and *meringue glacée*. He likes excellent ingredients, brilliantly cooked, but hold back on the sauces and the wine.

He will not necessarily turn up his nose at canned cat food. Manufacturers of assembly-line cat foods have been forced by competition rather than sentiment to improve their products. Those pretty tins of obnoxious barley-filled concoctions of unclassified odds and ends are now gathering dust on grocers' shelves. The fast movers are the identified flavors spiked with vitamins E, A, and C. You can buy kidney, heart, liver, salmon, and mackerel, and even a creamed tuna. The chicken, which you can serve your cat every Sunday, could double as a *pâté* for your hors d'oeuvre tray. All you need to do is add an anchovy.

Even in Europe, now, canned products are appearing with more and more frequency. The most sought-after brand in England is a tuna that must be pretty good because it is the staple diet of the beatnik set in Chelsea, and while they are Cats, they are not carnivorous quadrupeds.

Cats, as usual, have the last word on what *they* prefer and a survey of supermarket shelves proves that chopped kidney is the winner, paws down. Six cans of kidney sell to one of liver, and if this isn't a hint to one manufacturer, I don't know what is. His mackerel is mawkish, his heart too soggy, his chicken too overdone. His liver is so repulsive that one cat I know showed his disapproval by carrying it from his plate to his sandbox where he thought it belonged.

The vast majority of cats like any fish, from *gold* to *gefüllte*. Just go to a fish counter anywhere and take your pick. In France and Italy the markets stock every known species of their seas, rivers, and lakes. Rue de Buci, in Paris, is a traditional fish market, so is the Campo di Fiori in Rome. Irresistible are the mounds of oysters, mussels, and clams. Snails meander through seaweed, vermilion snappers share trays with robust cod and mackerel. Carp swim in cold water, and lobsters in hot. Marcel Pagnol characters will try to sell you a *loup de mer* or a *turbot*. *Resist*, please, if you are in a hotel. Cooking a *bouillabaisse* over a spirit lamp is too inconvenient, even to please a cat.

The *charcuteries* and grocery shops have a fine assortment of canned species. It's idiotic, I know, but sardines, salmon, and tuna, which are not native, are *imported*. It's more sensible to be conservative and use the local products. I've seen American canned salmon in Italy at a price that would make caviar look shabby. Please look for regional brands. Remember, *they* are *imported* when we are at home!

And remember, too, you have to do your figuring in the metric system. It's a good idea to study those front pages of the dictionary because you are through with pounds and tons once you cross the English Channel. It's really quite simple. Everything revolves around the *kilogram*. It takes time to learn not to refer to it as kilometer. (That's two thirds of a mile.) This kilogram is equal to 1000 grammes, which in turn equals two pounds five ounces with a few decimals left over. I made a lot of mistakes at first, but they amused my butcher so much, he called me *la belle américaine*, meaning, of course, dumb broad! In France, a *demi-kilo* and in Italy a *mezzo-kilo* are approximately one pound. You wouldn't dream of saying a quarter *kilo*, or an eighth of a kilo, so they invented grammes. Anything less than a half kilo is asked for in grammes. Butter, for instance, comes in 250- and 125-gramme packages, or half and one quarter pounds. A leg of lamb would weigh two kilos; so would a chicken. A small filet mignon, 160 grammes. One pound of sugar? A demi-kilo.

A cat with a normal appetite eats a half pound a day of whatever he eats. If he lives in Paris, *il mange* 250 grammes. Multiply it, divide it, subtract it, and it always comes out even. So much simpler than our complicated pounds and ounces, where we have to work with 32, 16, and 8, instead of nice zero numbers like 1000, 500, 100, and 10. My friends in England are already jittery about the future, when the U.K. joins the Common Market and the Sunday joint will weigh 3 kilos instead of six pounds. "It will never taste the same," they say. I hope it tastes better!

It took a long time for me to digest the information I just gave you. (It may *not* be Euclid correct, but it's accurate enough to feed yourself—and cat.) Just when I was a *succès fou* with the French butchers, I moved to Rome where they weigh things very peculiarly. No grammes here, although the kilo remains in wholes and halves as in France. There is a new word. Suddenly, it's a crazy mixed-up world of *ettos*. It was explained to me, so I'll try to tell you all about it. You must never say *cento grammi* (or *duecento,* or *trecento,* or *quattrocento*) in Rome, somebody might mistake you for a provincial from Milan. The 100-gram unit is always an *etto* and that's a little less than a quarter of a pound. You use *etto* up to four and then the fifth *etto* automatically becomes a *mezzo-kilo.*

A few months ago I stopped at a confectioner's in Milan to buy some of those divine *marrons glacés.* (God, are they marvelous! I'd send you some but they do not travel well.) I really only wanted two of them to eat immediately, so I asked for two *ettos'* worth. The shopkeeper looked at me with interest, then with pity in his voice said, "*Due etti?* Aha, *la bella romana!*" (Which means dumb broad from Rome.)

Oh, those continental butchers and *tripiers.* They are always closed when they should be open, but it's not for coffee breaks or assignations, it's tradition. I can save you a lot of time by trying to explain what is open and *when.* Continentals know how to live, and take a long siesta for lunch. People who sell meat are no exceptions; they have rigid rules and a complete understanding among themselves. You'll never find one butcher opening his shop at four when his competitors pull up their shutters at five. Maybe it's their union or guild, but the opening and closing hours are rigidly enforced.

Triperies and *boucheries,* in France, open their doors at about eight-thirty every morning, except Sunday. They stay that way, iron curtain up, until about twelve-thirty. *Then* the iron curtain is slowly rung down, but *not* all the way. As the hands of the clock turn toward one the curtain gets lower, with just enough room, at a quarter of, for some neglectful housewife to outrun time and get her calf's liver. What the butchers and *tripiers* do between the hours of one and five is none of our business, though a certain chambermaid I knew at the Lutèce is full of juicy gossip on the subject. At five the curtain goes up again, the pigs' heads and sides of beef take their places on the proscenium, and the dinner trade begins. Just one more hazard: everything in Paris closes *one* day each week.

Monday and Tuesday seem to be the favorites, although for anything but food shops, Saturday is very popular. If you don't know, then find out, because finding yourself on Rue Brea in front of a closed shop at eight-thirty in the morning is no way to start a week. But a sudden strike can keep them closed indefinitely. Read the newspaper. The French word for strike is *grève*. When you see that in a headline, read further. If it's only the Métro, your cat will eat, but if it's any other kind of transportation, supplies will get low rapidly. So hoard.

Hoard in Italy, too, because what you face there is the absolutely enormous number of national holidays and saints' days that close butcher shops (and everything else) so fast, you actually don't know where your next meal is coming from.

Well, Peg, I've just looked up from my typewriter and the sun is shining and there's a golden glow over the Borghese Gardens, so forgive me if I take Louis for a walk. I've lots more tips to give you, but they'll have to wait for the next rainy day.

With all my love,

BEULAH

CHAPTER TWELVE

Good Lord!
Still Another!

DEAR PEG:

I'm delighted that Kubla and Khan are doing so well and that some of my tips have been helpful. I *know* I didn't warn you about hot food. I should have. Cats like their food in that glorious temperature that is neither hot nor cold, neither lukewarm nor luke cold. The French have a word for it: *chambrée*—literally translated as chambered or more familiarly known as room temperature. (*Chambrée* is usually applied to wine, which should not be jolted out of its bouquet by iceboxes.)

I know *you* know that, Peg, because you *never* serve anything too cold. Only when you live out of the country do you realize the extent of the American love affair with ice. In Europe the *frig*, as we know it, does not exist. The European housekeeper shops twice a day for perishables, thus putting all the guilt for freshness or staleness on her purveyor.

Sometimes I have to have ice, and I can report that in Paris and Rome icemen still make their morning rounds with the huge twenty-five- and fifty-pound chunks that we knew as children. Winter provides its own icebox on the window sills of rich and poor alike.

The next time you are in Paris, just before the chestnuts are in blossom, or right after the last rose of summer, look up at the windows. In a few minutes you will lose count of all the milk bottles, legs of lamb, butter, cheese, and fruit you'll see in back of those eighteenth-century iron window grilles.

In any case, it comes to this. We may eat all the chilled melon or *vichyssoise* we wish, but *chambrée* everything you give to a cat.

Despite its fancy name, it's not so tough to do. Let us begin with food that has just been cooked—fish, for instance. Your cat is usually under your feet or on top of the stove, anxious for you to get it into his plate—*pronto!* Remove the fish from its cooking receptacle with a slotted spoon, place it in a colander or strainer, and run cold water over it. Boiled fish cools quickly and the sudden shower of cold water reduces it almost instantly to the perfection of *chambrée*. If you have the time (or if you have cooked the fish secretly) you may cool it naturally in its own juice.

Foods that have been stored in a refrigerator or on a window sill have to be brought up to the *chambrée* state too. Use *hot* water. A double boiler or a thin aluminum pan placed in the kitchen sink where the hot water is running is as good an idea as any. Aluminum conducts heat quickly so the food will heat in seconds if stirred with a fork. Just be sure that none of the hot water mingles with the food. Food heated this way is not cooked any more than you want it to be—it only *chambrées* things, the way we want them.

There are many ingenious methods of heating foods. In taking a motor trip, for instance, meat bought at roadside markets is either frozen stiff or just removed from a refrigerator. With a hungry cat in attendance, ready to tear the wrapping from his dinner, you must be careful to heat this "picnic" food as carefully as that served from a permanent kitchen. The space under the driver's seat seems to have exhaust pipes with no other function but to heat cats' food.

So much for hot and cold. Now about Kubla's passion for lamb kidneys and lamb kidneys alone. You've just got to learn to be a sneak, Peg, and con him into eating what you want him to. You either have to get up early in the morning to fool a cat, or you have to be a diplomat. Think of the story of the poor little unhappy midget who thought he was getting taller because some trickster with a macabre sense of humor cut an inch from the bottom of the midget's cane every week. You've just got to cut the bottom of Kubla's cane.

He obviously has a one-track mind. Simply put bits of what *you* think he should eat into what *he* thinks he should eat. Starting with only a tiny bite of the new food, you gradually increase the amount until your cat will be eating liver and calling it kidney, or eating kidney and calling it liver. Sometimes little tempters can make a cat investigate and taste a dish he has ignored for years. A dab of whipped cream, some melted butter can turn a formerly refused dish into a fetish.

You've got to be a sneak about other things too. Things like brewer's yeast, soybean oil, or olive oil, which are good for cats, are hard to administer if the cat thinks he's being dosed with medicine. We all know that suspicious look, don't we? For this underhand method, choose something your cat absolutely dotes on, then mix the added ingredient into the food. When I say mix, I mean mix. When you are through mixing, start mixing all over again until every particle of oil or yeast is hidden and absorbed. Kubla will never notice the foreign matter if he is hungry enough.

Now about his not drinking water. Well, Louis used to consider *water* a dirty five-letter word. But the vet said he had to drink it. Milk wasn't sufficient liquid. Certainly, I couldn't expect Louis to drink eight glasses of water a day, but a few laps he had to have, to flush his drainpipes. So water Kubla's milk. Increase the water and decrease the milk, until you end up with a slightly cloudy water bowl.

A lot of people put serious medications into a cat's food but I'd ask a vet about that because some worm medicines can be mixed with food, others not. (The atoms may combine into something desperate. Better worms than the risk of poisoning the cat.)

As for Khan being hungry all the time, what you want are between-meal snacks without calories. The French have a word for those unnecessary little tidbits we and they nibble—*amuse gueule.* This means literally "amuse mouth." They have no actual food value, unless, of course, you amuse your *gueule* with carrot sticks and other raw vegetables. You might call them a food supplement with nuisance value. After all, the elephant and the monkey in the zoo have their peanuts; we have ice cream sodas and chocolate bars. (Oh, what I'd give for one now!) The horse has his sugar and an occasional apple—the dog a bone. So why shouldn't pussy have something?

A cat, incapable of opening an icebox or a cookie jar, can't indulge in between-meal snacks without your co-operation. First on the list, a tested "good for the cat" biscuit—an offshoot of the classic dog biscuit. For cats the manufacturers have added fish or fish oils plus the usual bone meal, dehydrated vegetables, and a come-on flavor. Most cat owners admit that it never occurs to them to offer a cat dry food. Nonsense! Every cat I've known adores liver snips and fish balls and most of them even go for puppy biscuits in a big way. Caution though—cat biscuits have some uncertain directions for feeding on their packages. Nobody in his right mind would ever dream of giving a cat a handful of biscuits as a meal. This is what the manufacturers would like us to believe, but let them live their lives and let the cat live his!

No matter how you slice it, a biscuit is nothing but a snack. Some cats have a tendency to overdo things as far as tidbits are concerned, so disregard the suggestions on the package for feeding a handful at a time, just dole them out—a dollar down and a dollar a week. In this way, they'll stay down where they belong instead of reappearing suddenly when you want them least. Louis (and the Lord only knows where he got that idea) likes to have his biscuits on *my* bed, so the crumbs invariably found there are not always mine. The Dutch do a biscuit that is *divine* (or so I'm told), called Felix. Look for it in Paris, Rome, Madrid, and, of course, Rotterdam.

Corn kernels do a lot for a cat. Try giving him your used corncobs to chew on like a bone. A very funny sight indeed, but Khan won't notice your amusement. He'll be too busy chewing.

Cats are supposed to adore melons. I never saw a cat eat one but that doesn't mean he won't. I don't see why a nice ripe melon ball can't be offered to a cat. Even if he only rolls it under the stove, it gives him some exercise.

Prosciutto goes so well with melon that a strip of it, while you are having yours, might brighten a cat's otherwise dull day. Boiled ham and even bacon tickle a cat's palate, but like everything else that's good, it's tabu. Tabu or not, a sliver once in a while can do more good than harm, I always say.

Ham naturally leads to cheese. Cottage cheese has been given the blessing of the Better Cat Testing Bureau. Still, cottage cheese is a mild version of what the cheese world really has in store for cats. Every cat I know dotes on Bresse Bleue, Gorgonzola, Camembert, and anything else that smells, even Limburger. Cheese crumbs, and I mean *crumbs,* delight cats, but more than a crumb can turn a cat into a cheese lover, which may prove to be an expensive monkey on *your* back. Cheese is one of the things usually considered *not* good for a cat, but, after ten years of sampling everything from sapsago to mozzarella, the only bad effect I've noticed in Louis is a *grand soif.* And if cheese isn't good for a cat, water is!

My veterinary in Paris, Dr. Fourneau, suggested the most beneficial *amuse gueule* for man or beast. Melon seeds or pumpkin seeds, preferably. We can eat ours, he agreed, with the outer shell, salted, curried, spiced, or toasted, but the cat's ration must be removed from the outer shell and mixed with its food. Why? It's the most powerful vermifuge in the world. It may take an hour or so to shell a hundred melon seeds and be more than discouraging to realize that you have only a tablespoon of nut meats to show for your labor, but they chase worms on the double and are worth every moment of your effort.

Smoked oysters are really *amuse gueule*. I know a Burmese cat who began stealing them from hors d'oeuvre trays when she was two months old and has been eating them ever since with no apparent harm. Another cat I know thinks a matzoth ball is heaven on earth. She has one every Friday night and would gladly walk a tightrope across the Atlantic Ocean if one of her dumplings were on the other side.

Cats will nibble on nasturtiums, lily of the valley, rosebuds, carnations, papyrus, and philodendron, but will *not* eat lettuce, spinach, carrots, or parsley of their own free will. A cat who goes on a lily-of-the-valley eating spree is liable to go into shock as a result of too much digitalis (contained in those sweet-smelling blossoms) or suffer an ordinary indigestion from too much roughage.

Although Kubla and Khan may look pretty spectacular taking a bite out of a chrysanthemum, don't let them. Most flowers are as emetic as grass and only papyrus is a substitute for it. Papyrus with its long stem and classic hairy blossom end is so much part of ancient Egyptian hieroglyphics that I'm astounded every time I see it in my garden or in those of my neighbors. (*You* have a lovely batch of it on your hill.) It's good for cats, and the cat knows that instinctively.

Papyrus is a very amusing plaything too, and if it is regurgitated in a rather unrecognizable state, remember, this was the idea.

Leopard's blood, brewed originally for young kittens who thought they were still getting mother's milk, is adored by grown-up ones too. It looks and tastes just like melted vanilla ice cream without the vanilla. The recipe is patterned after Adele Davis' formula for tiger milk, which endows humans with excessive energy, good health and enough vitamins and minerals to sink a battleship. The pussy-cat version is actually the classic kitten-feeding formula with a few extra added attractions.

Here's what you do, Peg.

MIX TOGETHER:
1 can evaporated milk
an equal amount of boiling water
1 egg
1 tbs. corn syrup
1 tsp. brewer's yeast
1 tsp. soybean oil
(for kittens a few drops of cod-liver oil)

Beat with an egg beater. Serve immediately or refrigerate for future use. This amount makes about 1 pint.
Don't forget to *chambrée* before serving.

Adult cats who have long been off their two, five, and seven o'clock feedings enjoy leopard's blood as a snack and, whether they know it or not, it's good for them. It regulates innards, provides a wonderful between-meal snack, it gives sick cats and new mother cats a new lease on life. It can put weight on a thin cat and (*warning*) it can put weight on a fat cat too! To paraphrase the advertisement that used to be seen on all London buses, "Seven days make one *week*, leopard's blood makes one *strong!*"

After this long letter, darling, I need some myself. The picture's almost finished, and we should be coming home soon. Meanwhile, I'm preparing a cat cookbook[1] that you may find handy. If *you* think up any recipes, save them for me. Bless you, Peg, for letting me use you as a sounding board. I can hardly wait to see you, and introduce Louis to Kubla and Khan. Won't it be *hell* if they hate each other?

Love,

BEULAH

[1] See Appendix II.

CHAPTER THIRTEEN

The
Sandbox

They *loved* each other! Three such healthy fun-loving dolls! Except for Kubla's occasional tendency to biliousness. I knew I should have written Peg another letter about the awful fact that whatever goes into a cat must also come out. And I should address myself to the same subject here. But I'm shy. And this is a matter that is not considered polite.

Still, on television now, the digestive process is hinted at by the use of the word "regularity," and there is a good deal of praise for "pastel-colored tissues." (What the Prince in Rome would certainly have called a "euphemism.")

I'm afraid I must be blunter. For, if you travel with a cat, you must be prepared for a continuation of his natural functions or, heaven forbid, the lack of.

So let's face it squarely.

I paraphrase myself: what goes into one end of a cat doesn't *always* come out the other. Sometimes it exits at the entrance, other times it doesn't come out at all. Cats whose ladies' and gents' rooms are the great outdoors may keep their stopped-up plumbing a secret from you until it is too late. Too late is *too bad!*

The house cat whose sandbox is under daily supervision puts you in a much better position to evaluate daily performance. Sandboxes with nothing in them but sand can mean: your cat has formed a new habit and is using the bookshelves, bidet, clothes closet, bathtub, or toilet. Perhaps the sandbox isn't cleaned often enough to suit his fastidious tastes. Perhaps he's just "ornery." Perhaps he

5.

James Dean with Louis.

6.

Visiting Colette.

Walking with Igor Stravinsky.

8.
De Chiricho used an old-fashioned remedy to keep Louis quiet.

9.

Blaise Cendrars managed
to prevent a fight between
his famous dog, Wagon Lit,
and Louis.

10. Georges Braque thought Louis' colors very like Braque colors.

11.

Picasso admired Louis but preferred to be photographed with
one of his doves.

12.

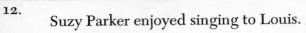

Suzy Parker enjoyed singing to Louis.

13.

Cocteau and the prop that shattered Louis' poise.

14.

Cary Grant approved Louis' diet.

isn't well. Perhaps he isn't using it because he *can't*. Urine stoppage is much more serious than constipation and it can mean a critical kidney disorder with death just around the corner.

Don't scold a cat if he leaves wet spots—just be glad that they're *wet*.

Bowel stoppage can be caused by any number of things, but usually it's just a case of a sluggish constitution or hair balls. When the cat swallows thousands of hairs a day by grooming his coat something happens to him that shouldn't happen to anybody. The accumulation of this mass causes what can be described as a felt cigar to form in the intestinal tract. When the hair ball can neither come up nor go down, a crisis occurs, and this is the time cats mutter their so beautifully named (by Colette) *Hymn to the Doorknob*.

A cat knows a lot more about his innards than you do, and that incessant plaint may be his way of asking for *grass*. When an apartment cat asks for grass, he may not get it and the time will come soon when urban residents will take a gentle hint from the French and keep little pots of grass available at all times.

Veterinarians vary in their opinion of grass for cats and some-day they will battle it out in the Coliseum with cats applauding from the bleachers. Grass is a cat's cider vinegar, bicarbonate of soda, his little liver pills, his milk of magnesia, and his peppermint tea. You don't have to go to the Berlitz School to understand cat language. His demand for grass is unmistakable.

Wherever we (my cat and I) are, grass is somewhere, but my cat can't always get to it. That *folle de Chaillot* seen picking stray blades on Avenue Kléber is I. The woman in black, on her knees, in the meadow of Central Park, pulling up sprouts, is the willing pupil of a competent teacher. I can pick and choose with the rest of the felines. Through a process of elimination, I have actually identified the types of grass cats need. I have taken samples to a plant nursery and bought the corresponding seeds. Rye grass is most popular with my cat, so I've strewn it throughout my garden. Seeds planted in mild weather come up in about a week. In England, the Cat Protective League sells you seeds and instructions for grow-ing them indoors. Indoor grass is much finer than outdoor grass. It's cleaner, too. The vulgar name for the most popular grass is cocks-foot, but the botanical name is much nicer—*Dactylis glomerata*.

Unscientifically, of course, grass seems to do two things. By some mysterious abrasive action it causes (but not always) a regurgitation. Perhaps a gas pocket that has been disturbing the cat is relieved. Sometimes the cat will bring up the grass in a few minutes after he has eaten it, in a colorless liquid. At other times it releases something rather horrifying if the cat has eaten his dinner before the grass. Once in a while a hair ball will come up and the cat is perfectly content. I suggest that owners of *indoor* cats watch them thoroughly after grass has been ingested. The forthcoming upheaval may come at any time—anywhere! It's best that they be confined to an easily washable area such as a bathroom or kitchen, because a cat will always *choose* a bedspread or Aubusson rug if left to his own devices.

It's been said that a cat is the most constipated creature in the world. I suppose there are some talented people who can give a cat an enema or a suppository, but I am not one of them. When a constipation crisis occurs, and this *is* a crisis, I take the coward's way out and rush my cat to a veterinary. The veterinary knows where everything is and belongs under a cat's tail. My veterinary relaxes the cat first with a mild sedative that helps the elimination muscles to function normally with no tension. Whether he resorts to enema or suppository I do not know, but an hour later Louis is ready and very happy.

Dr. Michael Miller, my veterinary in Los Angeles, has a special gook that prevents constipation if administered regularly. Regularly means once a week, constipation or not, on an *empty* stomach. And don't think *that's* easy.

It takes quite a bit of researching to discover when a cat's stomach is empty. You can assume that the predawn hour, eight hours after he has eaten his last food, is the time. (If during the night he has consumed a cashmere sweater and the northeast corner of a rug, that is *his* business.)

So administer the gook, which has the consistency of vaseline, the look of a melted caramel, the odor of molasses. Cats won't admit it, but they don't mind the stuff at all. Put about a teaspoon of it on a finger, get the cat to open his mouth, and spread it over the roof. Close his mouth at once. He will gulp and swallow and spend the next hour washing the signs of it from his whiskers.

The action of this medication takes place about eight hours later and its results are worth all the trouble it took. Between you and me, I've discovered pure white vaseline does the same thing. The

trick in administering both of these panaceas is the tact and surprise element involved. I wouldn't blame a cat in the least if he
heads for the nearest hideout once he sees you reach for the vaseline
jar.

Gourmandizing will clog plumbing as often as hair balls and,
paradoxically, grass will occasionally cause what it is trying to cure.
Certain foods have laxative properties, and when a cat is over
seven he might have to resort to including liver (raw), brains, and
milk in his diet a few times a week.

Warning! You can't get away with putting vaseline, gook, or
mineral oil in a cat's food. It will interfere with digestion and make
a cat suspicious of even the choicest cut of round steak in the
future. If you are a coward and must dose a cat in his food, then
add some olive oil (the kind from sardines is fine) or some soybean
oil, perhaps a tablespoon to a dinner serving. Soybean oil is an
adequate lubricant and contains a large amount of vitamin E, which
helps coats glisten and puts the spirit of youth into old cats. If a
cat turns his nose up at a plate of oil-soaked food, forget the whole
thing, and sob.

Another warning: cats hate the sight of an empty plate. Although
I know it's against the rules to leave uneaten food around for more
than half an hour, I was too weak in spirit "at the beginning" to
enforce the law. I feel that cats enjoy eating when they *want*
to eat. It may take hours for a slow eater to finish a bowl of food.
A "bolter" may polish it off in a few minutes and probably bring
it right up.

You wipe it right up.

By this time you've discovered that, to paraphrase Tennessee Wil-
liams, "A cat is not filled with rose petals." Neither is he stuffed with
sugar and spice and all things nice. People call cats' and dogs'
eliminations all sorts of silly things like "messing" or "dirtying"
—"duty" or *"making a remark"*—even in France, *"besoins."* In New
York City animals "commit nuisances" officially in the privacy of
their own homes, but the same act accomplished on the sidewalk
imposes a fine—and that goes for cats too.

A cat would rather die than commit its nuisance in public view,
or at least leave it in public view for more than a few seconds.
Have you ever noticed how frustrated the lions and tigers are in a
zoo cage with nothing more than hard, unpenetrating cement on
which to attend to their natural functions? They claw and try to

make themselves believe they are in a jungle clearing scratching up plant debris and sand to cover their tracks and preserve their scent from their enemies. A cat, too, demands and should have the proper facilities to exercise his jungle rights. The sandbox placed strategically in a home is the answer to the problem. The street cat, of course, has no problem.

Louis, who is about as far from a street cat as you can get, uses an 11" by 14" white enameled developing tray filled with litter[1] as his convenience while he is at home. (He is, after all, a photographer's cat.) For travel, my inventive husband designed a monument to cat comfort, a car carrier with gents' room attached.

We originally bought a number of ready-made and thoroughly unsatisfactory quonset hut cases made of some sort of laminated wood. (What *is* laminated wood?) Buying a case for a cat without the cat is like guessing at the stocking size of the girl next door. Three cases purchased at various pet shops guaranteed to fit an adult Siamese proved to do just that—they *just* fit him, which won't do at all. We were thus forced to smuggle Louis into the Farmer's Market, which has one of the best pet supply shops in the world— and doesn't admit pets. (Go figure it out.) A patient clerk with a vast knowledge recommended the one we finally bought—the size for overweight Scotties. It has a curious bunched-up look, but to hell with aesthetics. We took it, even though it exceeded our weight budget. Once the case was ours, we rushed to a metal shop with a floor plan and a rendering of what my husband had cooked up. The metalworker blanched at the amateur blueprint. As a pigeon fancier, he nourished an abiding distrust of cats. But his pride in craft finally prevailed, and he reluctantly undertook the challenge, brightening visibly as we enthusiastically adored his amendments.

The finished case he came up with was one we had dreamed about. He soldered aluminum runners to the floor into which slid a rustproof pan two inches high and exactly the length and width of the carrier. As easy as pie, the pan could be drawn out of the runners and deposited anywhere, publicly or privately, for Louis to use. I always kept a token amount of litter in it. (Warning: any more than just that adds to its weight and leaves traces.)

It's important the portable gents' room be a well-concealed secret in transit. The first thing to do when entering a hotel room (*yes,*

[1] Processed ground clay

the first thing!) is to remove the sandbox, install it in the bathroom (or reasonable facsimile), and show Louis where it is. He quickly catches on. (Once in a while, at home, when I feel he is nostalgic for Paris or Rome, I take the old sandbox out and let him imagine that he's somewhere near the Etoile.)

As for packaged cat box litter, until recently it was strictly something you could buy in the U.S.A., and you had to carry it along with you, if you wouldn't use alternatives. In Rome, in 1962, I saw a package called *Katzen* something or other, a West German version of our domestic variety. It's around Europe, but still rare. *Sans* litter, you have to resort to torn paper, sand, ashes, or sawdust. Paper and sand stay moist a long time and too amply advertise the fact that you have a cat; even Patou's Joy can't muffle the evidence.

Ashes spread less propaganda, but they are a little hard to come by these days, so sawdust remains a loser's choice. It is very easy to get, slightly deodorizing, and so cheap that you can change twice a day. A shoeboxful is a day's ration, five pounds should last a week.

In Paris, the Cat Capital of the World, wouldn't you know they'd put sawdust up in pretty paper bags with Minou's picture on it? These lovely packages are for sale *only* in *drogueries* or *marchands des couleurs*—both fancy names for old-fashioned hardware stores. Sawdust in France is called *sciure*, and it's very hard to pronounce. Write it down and hand it to the man. In Paris you'll usually get some.

Outside of Paris (and Lyons and Bordeaux), you'll have to roam about in lumberyards, *chez* the carpenter, in cafés, or your own hotel. To avoid this, if you're driving, stow a couple of bags in the trunk. Good for ballast, too. If you're flying, the law of diminishing returns sets in.

The first time I arrived in Paris with Louis, I wished I *had* brought along my own sawdust. It was eight o'clock of a pink spring evening, and Paris was never lovelier or more romantic. My husband and I were eager to dine and walk on the Champs Elysées, but first we had to attend to Louis. But how? No litter, no sand, no sawdust, nothing more than a few partisan newspapers. And we knew torn newspaper was out of the question. Louis can never resist playing with it to the exclusion of the serious business for which it's intended.

All the *drogueries* were closed. I tried to reach cat-owning friends with no success. Then my husband remembered the delightful pet shops situated along the Quai de la Mégisserie that sell everything from chipmunks to cheetahs, and supplies to make them happy. It's a delight to stroll at night along the Seine, browsing the linnets, rhesus monkeys, birdcages, myriad varieties of millet and grains, white mice, black cats, emerald parrots, and goldfish. Yes, they are open until nine and they *do sell* everything to make a pet happy.

So out I went to the quai to discover that they do indeed sell everything imaginable—everything *but sciure. Cherchez la droguerie!*

Distrait, I was about to *chercher* when I noticed a barrel of white sand. A good substitute, I thought, at least just for a day. A sign said it was sold by the hundred *grammes,* or approximately the quarter pound. I asked for two *kilos* and the clerk gasped. He kept shaking his head as he filled a sack and handed it to me. I said, *"Combien, monsieur?"*

And he said, "Thirty-five francs." (New francs, of course.)

"Seven dollars for a pound of sand!" I was aghast!

Oh, but not just ordinary sand, he explained, but white coral sand from the remotest reef in remotest Tahiti, of a texture, of a magnificence so rare, so *recherché,* so exquisite, that only the most exclusive tropical fish, in the *most* exclusive aquariums of Paris, deserved it in their tanks, and only a handful at that.

What do you think I did? I bought it, that's what I did. And used it until we went to Italy.

In Italy, sawdust becomes *segatura,* and it is sold in any establishment that provides charcoal, wood, washing soap, and crockery. On a rainy day in Rome sawdust is used by the ton to make the tile or marble floors in cafés, restaurants, and food shops less slippery. Since it rains quite a lot in Rome, the sawdust supply is always at its peak. The little stores that purvey sawdust at decent prices are in dark holes in the basements of buildings.

On the other hand, sawdust profiteers have normal shops adorned by an assortment of repulsive candy-pink and nile-green plastic shopping baskets and bread trays. Practically every neighborhood has one and when you come to know the owners of the shops you will find them to be charming, friendly, and black marketeers at heart. For enough lire they are ready to do anything for you but give you a container for your sawdust. Bring your own!

If you've millions, the pet shop on Via Frattina in Rome sells the

German version of cat box litter in five-pound sacks. They not only give you a container but tie the package with ribbon.

Litter, ashes, and sawdust are all very well, but don't forget the greatest treat in a city cat's life is the opportunity to "scratch" on a beach or in the soft earth often found in vineyards. Choose an area in which the grapes are already picked to be sure you're not desecrating the autumn crop. Farmers are not broad-minded in this area. One threatened me with a German Luger. I retreated, though I'm sure it wasn't loaded. He was wearing such a sweet horse's hat.

Conrad Hilton may now draw *his* Luger. While the Madrid Hilton was under construction, we were staying at the Crillon, just opposite. The building site was a relief map of lovely mounds of sand and earth, for which Louis lusted. How could I deny him this only free available soil in Spain, east of the Basque coast? In any case, we (I mean he) used it three times a day, concentrating chiefly on the sand used in mixing the cement for the hotel walls. It's been petrified, of course, but there can be no question it's there.

I apologize, Mr. Hilton. Before you get too angry, remember they say it's good luck!

It's even better luck when your cat discovers the bathtub. Don't scold him. It's a great occasion. Break out the flag and rejoice. My husband opened a bottle of Dom Perignon. *I* opened a can of imported cleanser. Works fine. I'm told some educated cats actually use the toilet. I doubt if they are educated enough to flush it.

What a cat really likes (at least Louis does) in a European bathroom is that installation that American tourists refer to (most generously) as a *thing*, and use as a fruit bowl, a laundry tub, or a foot bath, superciliously ignoring its built-in purpose. Louis fits right into this superbly shaped device and enjoys a nap in it immensely.

I never disturb him unless it's absolutely *urgent*—I mean, unless I have absolutely no other place to put my *Reine Claudes*.[2]

2 Plums.

CHAPTER FOURTEEN

Jimmy
Dean

Plums are a rather old-fashioned fruit, and have scarcely any
admirers left. Still, I dote on them, and so did Jimmy Dean, the
young actor who skyrocketed to instant and terrible fame, and died
too soon. He had a plum tree in his garden out in the valley—a
Satsuma—that bore bushels of fruit. That's how we became friends.

One day my husband called me from Warner Brothers.

"Do you mind if I bring a kid home to dinner? He's working in
Giant. What do we have?"

"Curried chicken, and if he's a kid he'll hate it. What's his name?"

"Jimmy Dean."

I gulped and rushed to put on a strawberry facial mask.

So Jimmy crossed our threshold, that early summer evening, for
the first time. My husband introduced us; he seemed sullen, unfriendly, and so very young. I have few ways to communicate with
the very young. But Louis has many, and he saved the day by jump-
ing into the boy's lap. Jimmy held him very tight, and I worried
about that, but thank heaven, Louis did not protest, but purred—
and they were fast and instant friends.

A good thing, too, because Jimmy had Louis on his knee all
through dinner, which, candor compels me to report, was far from
a success. Jimmy hated the curry and the condiments, especially
the Bombay duck and the coconut.

"Coconut on meat?" he asked incredulously.

His palate was attuned to hamburgers and chili—but he did like
the Major Grey chutney.

"Hey," he said. (It seemed to me then that he began every sentence with hey.) "Hey, it tastes like my grandma's plum preserve back in Indiana. Do you ever make plum preserves? I got a lot of plums. I love plums."

"Me too," I said.

"Hey, I'll bring you some tomorrow."

So he did.

The entire crop of his abundant tree was deposited at my back door in crates, bushel baskets, and cartons. For the next few days I turned the Satsumas into jam, jellies, pies, and even did something with ginger, chili peppers, and cardamom to make them taste like his grandma's preserves back in Indiana.

He was, from that time forward, a constant guest—sometimes invited, sometimes not—but always welcome. I cannot tell you whether he came to see my husband or myself. Yes, I can; he liked us but he loved Louis and we came to recognize that he was Louis's guest. And Louis was a good host. He let Jimmy sit in his throne. The throne was (and still is) an eighteenth-century Venetian chair, scarred by the many indiscretions of Doge and cat. Created for aristocrats in brocades and laces, the chair seemed to be outraged by the intrusion of Jimmy's long blue-jeaned legs. It was here, in this awkward position, the chair creaking under him, that he fell asleep with Louis on his lap. And the two of them dreamed together.

Jimmy dreamed, perhaps, of Fairmount, Indiana, and the farm that he loved, or the vague shadow of a mother who was taken from him early in life. Or he may have indulged in his recurrent fantasy of walking down the Boulevard St. Germain. It was a street he knew well from photographs. It was a dream that was never to come true.

Too often Jimmy Dean has been described as a meteor, a crazy mixed-up kid, a poet, and a great Dane puppy. He was all of those and at the same time none. His laugh was a half-silent chuckle, as though exuberance embarrassed him. His enthusiasms ran through the spectrum of human interests: motorcycles to serious music, jazz to bullfighting, apple pie to cats.

Despite this diversity of interests, and a lack of formal education, he had the austere good sense of a Quaker and the defense mechanisms of a turtle. In this case the carapace was his own private world, a world of Bartok and Schoenberg, the primitive African beat, the polished steel innards of a racing car, and the writers he had only recently discovered: Sartre, Genet, and Malaparte. I couldn't be sure whether his interest in them was intellectual pretense or valid. After a while, it seemed to me, they did one thing at least—ignited in Jimmy an irrepressible desire to see Paris, Rome, and Venice. More than anything else in the world, he wanted to take off for Europe.

He couldn't because, paradoxically, he was *too* successful. He had far too many motion picture commitments. In no time at all he had become big business, besieged by offers, suffocated in contractual commitments. When the contracts were honored he was planning to go abroad—perhaps live there and, in living there, find himself. But for the present he had to make do with a world he never made or lived in—a world he saw only through picture and travel books—and, it seemed, very little human contact. I know little of his personal life (he was the least self-revealing human being I've ever met), but there appeared to be an emptiness, a curious gossamer curtain between him and the world.

There was no curtain between him and cats. And so he decided that he must have one—one as close to Louis as possible. He asked me to help him find a Siamese. We pored over the ads in the newspapers and finally we came across a likely one in Venice—in Venice, California, that is.

It's a curiously depressing place, Venice, California, conceived by an imaginative but tasteless real estate developer in the early part of this century as a rank imitation of Venice, Italy, and a ranker imitation never existed. At one time there were water-filled canals with cheery little gondolas floating, piloted by ersatz gondoliers, and an occasional California replica of the Rialto Bridge, but no longer. There are still canals in the latter-day Venice, but they're dry and full of refuse—and the streets teem with an odd tribe of bearded beatniks and black-stockinged girls.

Their idol was Jimmy Dean. And yet Jimmy and I went to Venice to a little old California bungalow, to the house of an elderly lady with purple hair, a batik dress, and a Spanish comb, and there we negotiated the purchase of the most beautiful, perfectly made little Siamese kitten you could possibly want, and we walked through the streets looking at old Venice together, and nobody—but nobody —recognized Jimmy Dean.

He was the young movie star over whom teen-age girls screamed and swooned and in whose pattern teen-age boys molded them-

selves. Still nobody recognized him as we walked back to his car—
a racing Porsche, about which I try not to think.

And then Jimmy pointed to the St. Mark Hotel and he told me
that Christopher Isherwood had told *him* that Sarah Bernhardt had
once stayed there.

So Jimmy and his kitten and I went into the St. Mark and asked
the room clerk if he would show us the room in which Sarah Bernhardt had once stayed. He looked at us blankly and called the
owner, and Jimmy tipped him a few dollars, and we were ushered
upstairs to the corner salon where once the divine Sarah had lived.
It was grimy now, but you could see that once it had been elegant and worthy.

The bed was brass and the clerk assured us it was the very one
in which Madame had slept. So Jimmy and his kitten lay down on
the bed, and he closed his eyes very tight, and I found myself a
little embarrassed. Was this boy really trying to invoke an ancient
spirit to make him a better actor? And was this kitten somehow a
part of the invocation?

"Come on, Jimmy," I said. "Let's get out of here. It's a flea trap."

He was angry with me.

But not for long. He called me three and four times a day to
find out what to do with his kitten—and Dr. Spock himself couldn't
have taken better care of a baby.

He measured out his food, took his temperature, used a ruler to
see if he were growing properly, examined his sandbox to make certain there were no worms, took him to the veterinarian at regular
intervals, held him while he had his shots, built him a bed and then
let him sleep on his own, loved him, cherished him, spoiled him,
wrapped his life around him.

This boy, who could have had his pick of any girl in the world,
who could have dined at the great houses, who could have lived
it up, preferred a little Siamese kitten. His only complaint was that
he had to get up so early.

"Hey, I like to sleep late, Beulah," he told me.

"Then sleep late," I said. "You can afford it."

"But how can you with a cat?" he insisted. "I mean, sometimes
I mean I really wonder whether it's worth having a cat, he makes
you get up so early. Wish you'd never talked me into him."

"You can always give him away," I said testily.

"Give him away?" said Jimmy.

"Yes," I said. "I know somebody who's dying for a little Siamese. Very responsible people. Give him a good home."

"Have you got rocks in your head?"

"No, Jimmy. I'm just trying to help you out."

"It doesn't sound like that."

"All I mean is if you *really* want to get rid of the cat . . ."

"Get rid of him?" His voice was filled with horror. "I'd rather die. Hey, I love him the most of anything in the world."

I think that was a simple truth. In his terrible loneliness (I am not a psychiatrist so I cannot tell you why he was so lonely), the only friend he really had was a little Siamese kitten.

So you see, if cats do nothing else, give them this much: they comfort and warm the introverted.

CHAPTER FIFTEEN

Colette

The introverts and the intellectuals of the world agree, as
though by some international manifesto, that they are pro-cat. They
may differ in their opinions of Impressionism, Dadaism, Cubism,
dialectics, James Joyce, and women, but their love and respect for
the cat are unanimous.

I may be chauvinistic in my attitude toward France, but I do
claim that *chatisme*[1] has reached the zenith of perfection there.
To a Frenchman, the cat, a non-conformist, a revolutionary, and an
intransigent, is the symbol of *Liberté, Egalité, Fraternité.* The
French have dedicated poems, essays, plays, and great works of
art to them, extolled their virtues, set them up as paragons, and
only infrequently criticized their shortcomings. The cult of *chatisme*
is propagandized so capably that even cat-hating iconoclasts and
infidels, finding themselves among the alien corn, are forced to re-
treat into philosophical and erudite attack. It is not the cat they
deplore; it is the *idea* of the cat.

Conversely, it is the *idea* of the cat that Richelieu, Baudelaire,
Hugo, Steinlen, Anatole France, Jean Cocteau, Lenore Fini, and
Colette have extolled, surrounded by an entire Larousse Encyclo-
pedia of common people who have helped temper the climate of
France to the taste of the cat. No wonder the French cat continues
to purr so contentedly on the painter's easel, the poet's knee, the
writer's table.

And so we come to Colette and the first time I met her. By then,
her writing table had no cat on it. She was aging and too ill to
give a cat proper care, but her enthusiasm remained. It was perhaps the simple word *chat* in my letter to her that caused her

[1] A word I've made up for the occasion.

to answer it immediately, asking me to telephone for an appointment.

I had never "hunted" a celebrity before and the Lord knows I've been professionally exposed to them for years. Colette was different. I not only admired her as a writer, but to me she was the reincarnation of Bast, the cat goddess. Certainly she was Queen of all Cats, Empress of Felines, and an Honorary Cat. My husband wanted to photograph her. I wanted to meet her and have her stroke Louis.

One day as I strolled through the Palais Royal gardens, my eye was attracted to an upper floor along the north entrance. An ashen face, framed in a shock of vermilion hair, was looking down into the garden at some children playing hide-and-go-seek. It was Colette. My eye caught hers and I mumbled an embarrassed *"Bon jour."* She smiled and waved at me. Perhaps she thought she knew me. I am shy, no matter what *you* think, so I accelerated my step and headed for the arcades, out of her sight.

I thought about it later and decided that I was an ass: I had missed the opportunity of my life by not continuing my *bon jour* into a conversation. But I comforted myself with the fact that at least I had *seen* Colette. That should have been enough for any upstart from Brooklyn. No matter how I looked at it, I was ahead, for it was indeed a far cry from the Colette shelf in the public library to actually seeing her in Paris.

About two years later my husband became quite well known as a photographer. He had by that time photographed most of the great men and women of arts and letters in Paris as a preparation for the book he was to do with Aldous Huxley, *The French of Paris.* We had already worked with Jean Cocteau, Matisse, Chagall, Picasso, Jacques Villon, Vlaminck, Utrillo, Marie Laurencin, Paul Elouard, and Léger, but no book on Paris would have been complete without Colette. Somehow we saved her for the last. Both of us retained that childish habit of looking forward to dessert, and Colette was the chocolate soufflé.

I decided to write a letter to Colette, rather than telephone. She could answer my letter or not without embarrassment if she felt too ill to see us. I told her of our wish to photograph her and casually mentioned the fact that we had a cat with us who would very much like to meet her too. I omitted the banalities of being a great admirer of hers, hoping that when she read that I had brought a cat from America it would be a case of *"ça va sans dire."*

Actually I never thought she would answer my letter. It was an
infringement of the privacy of not only a world-famous celebrity
but a very ill one. Perhaps her vanity (she *was* vain) would prevent her from agreeing to be photographed now that she was aging.

The very next day I found a mauve envelope in my mailbox. It
was a letter from Colette and it read:

CHERE MADAME:

*Je suis immobilisée depuis longtemps par une longue et doulour-
euse arthrite des jambes, mais dès que vous serez arrivés je vous
recevrai tous les trois, et contente de vous voir. Téléphonez-moi à
Gutenberg 61.36. Surtout n'oubliez pas le chat Louis! Je n'ai plus
de chats, je suis trop âgée. Mais personne ne les connaît ou ne
les aime mieux que moi!*

Croyez que je suis affectueusement à vous,

COLETTE
9 *Rue Beaujolais*[2]

So I instantly called Gutenberg 61.36, made an appointment,
and then went feverishly to work.

There was a lot to do. Louis had to be brushed. A basket had to
be found for him, too. His old traveling case was rapidly beginning
to look like Flea Market luggage. The concierge of the hotel, so impressed with our invitation from Colette, contributed a slightly used
champagne basket, which I suppose is the traditional container for
kittens in France. Unfortunately, Louis's cubic footage was much
more than the basket's, so he had to make the voyage to Rue Beaujolais half in and half out. The idea was to present Louis to Colette in the basket, so that *she* might open the lid herself. This was
a little theatrical, I know, but it seemed more gala and more appropriate to the occasion than having Louis on my shoulder.

Anyone seeing us enter the doorway of 9 Rue Beaujolais that day
would have identified us as picnickers. I, carrying a basketful of
Louis, plus an overwhelming bouquet of yellow roses and a bottle

[2] DEAR MADAM:
   I have been incapacitated for a long time by long and severe arthritis of the legs,
but, as soon as you arrive, I will receive all *three* of you, and happy to see you.
Telephone me at Gutenberg 61.36. Above all, don't forget the cat, Louis. I have no
more cats, I am too old. But nobody knows them or loves them better than I.
   Believe that I am affectionately yours,

COLETTE
9 Rue Beaujolais

of wine. My husband, weighted down with his camera case, a tripod, and a box of photographs to show Colette.

Pauline, her housekeeper and friend, opened the door for us. "Hurry, Madame is waiting. She hasn't slept all night thinking about your cat."

From a room far to my right I heard: "Have they come?"

"Yes, madame."

"Is the cat there?"

"Yes, madame."

"Hurry them in here!"

I could hardly believe it was actually Colette's voice. I wanted to hear more of it, the rolling *rr*s in her pronunciation of *arrivés,* the guttural *chat,* so full of love and expectation. I felt at that moment that nowhere in France would that simple four-letter word *chat* be given such homage. Neither at the Comédie Française, nor at the Académie. It was as though the word belonged to Colette and to the world of cats.

In a few minutes I was standing next to her day bed, lowering my head to receive her kiss, but her impatient eyes focused on the champagne basket.

"What have you in there? Champagne?" It was a little game, for what was in the basket was obvious from the muffled miaowing complaints.

Colette, her hair now gray, her limbs immobilized by arthritis, lay on her couch in her little study. Her worktable, littered with manuscripts, pen pots, a wine bottle and glasses, and one beautiful rose in a small vase, lay across her knees. She faced the wall lined with bookshelves and her famous collection of glass paperweights. At her left, a window framed the tops of the trees in the garden below. Red silk curtains gave the room a rosy glow and, despite the odor of beeswax that Pauline used to burnish the old woods, I detected the faint smell of cats, and unquestionably Louis did too.

"Let me have him," insisted Colette.

I opened the lid and Louis jumped right on Colette's bed and found her lap, and nestled, but I did *not* think, comfortably. Her hands expertly stroked his coat, like those of the blind exploring a page of Braille. She traced his ears, his jaw, his moist nose, his back, and his tail with her long fingers. She felt the quiet pulsation of his heart, the muscles in his legs, and then moved her head back slightly so that her farsighted eyes could better estimate his coloring.

"Oh, Monsieur Louis! How well dressed you are!" It was the verdict of a peer. The opinion of an expert judge, an unqualified expert. The only trouble was that Louis had a funny look on his face, and I thought I must grab him, but I didn't dare, for my husband's camera by now was almost silently recording the scene.

"Vrouvrouvrou," Colette purred. Louis rubbed his ears against her arm.

"Mirrououou?" questioned Colette.

"Currrououl!" answered Louis.

And so the conversation continued until a small pigeon alighted on her window sill. At that moment Colette reached out to embrace Louis, but he, intrigued by the bird movement so close to him, responded to his natural reflexes. He scratched and bit Colette.

Pauline screamed.

My husband turned white.

Louis retreated to a corner.

I felt the earth go out from under me at the enormity of this scandal. All my love for Louis turned to hate, and I would cheerfully have strangled him. But that didn't seem the thing to do, even if I could have caught him.

What in the name of all the forty French immortals *does* one do? What *do* you say when your cat bites the fragile hand of Colette? You do what I did. You scream, "Oh, madame! He never did that before!" You lie as you've never lied before, because you know deep down in your deepest heart that he *has* done that before—not only to Colette but to Edward who delivers the groceries (who only smiled), to Arbit Blatas, the painter (who threatened suit), to your best friend in Rome, Princess Rachel Starroba (who went instantly to Lausanne for treatment), and, while you're going through the casualty list, you add yourself (who has never admitted it to a living soul before).

Only Colette remained calm. She pushed aside Pauline's attempts to wash the wound with an antiseptic, lit a cigarette, and addressed herself directly to Louis, who with uncommon touchiness had his back turned on her.

"Good day," she said. Her voice was not icy. Nor could you say it was warm.

My "good day" was hoarse and shaky.

Hoarser and shakier, a few days later, when *l'affaire Louis* became front-page news. Colette was interviewed by Claude Gregory in *Arts*, the weekly newspaper consecrated to happenings in the literary and art world. Monsieur Gregory obviously wanted Madame Colette's views on her appointment to the Goncourt Academy, but she had something else in mind.

The interview, as it appeared in *Arts*, was this, literally translated:

COLETTE:

Too bad you came so late, Monsieur Gregory. Two days ago my apartment had Louis XIV and the sun. Tomorrow perhaps another ray of sunshine will appear, but not Louis XIV, no, no more. Louis XIV is a cat of America who rushed himself here to see me before going on an extended tour of the museums and art galleries of Europe. Imagine, coming to see *me!* Such an important cat!

PAULINE:
(*interjecting*)
But he scratched you, madame! Remember?

COLETTE:

Yes, Pauline, I myself remember. I hereby apologize to him publicly. It was my fault. I should have known better than to keep a cat from doing what he wanted to do. I held him against his will. It is I who was guilty, not *he*.

I sent Madame Colette a wisp of a shawl from Dior. She sent me a copy of her collected novels.

There will never be another like her.

CHAPTER SIXTEEN

Picasso

Or like Picasso.

I remember so well the early November morning he agreed to receive us. Paris was shrouded in that peculiar icy atmosphere that penetrates your bones like a darning needle. The cold and the damp vied to see which could make you more miserable. Life away from a sizzling radiator or a hot stove was not to be considered. We rarely left our hotel room in weather like that, so it had to be this great event—the rendezvous to photograph Pablo Picasso—to get us out onto the damp streets. Still, we were not in the best of humors.

The apartment building where the Great Man lives on Rue des Grands Augustins looked ordinary enough and not formidable, but when you started to climb the iron staircase you made a mental note never to trust the looks of a façade. Up and up you went, one steep flight, two steep flights, three steep flights, not entirely encouraged along the way by the printer's forefinger that directed you with one word: PICASSO.

The stairs seemed endless and on every fourth one I caught the scent of whole generations of cats. Interesting, of course, but my one objective now was that little door, way, way up where *he* was waiting for Louis, my husband, and myself.

Don't think you can ring the doorbell and be admitted to Picasso's studio, just like that. Not at all, for behind that door was and is Jaime Sabartes, Picasso's good friend, secretary, and all-around watchdog. He guards Picasso with the ferocity of a starving Doberman and he appears to have the same kind of disposition until you know him. Not that *that's* easy.

When Monsieur Sabartes says, "Who is it?" you'd better be somebody he is expecting, or you will be descending those steep stairs in record time. But if Sabartes knows you, or at least has arranged an appointment for you, he will open the door and welcome you graciously into the *maître's* sanctum sanctorum.

He opened the door and welcomed us. He was charming, but not very.

Somewhere a stew was cooking. The perfume of garlic and red wine permeated the air, but it was nearly obliterated by the smells of linseed oil and fresh paint. No wonder! We were completely surrounded by canvases, some large, some small. And all Picassos.

From above, I could have sworn I heard the sound of cooing doves. It was my imagination working overtime, I assured myself, since there were doves all around me on canvases, lithographs, book covers, in bronze, and on posters.[1]

While we talked to Sabartes until Picasso should appear, Louis took a few moments to do a little exploration on his own. Under a table, he saw a huge black folio, completely covered with dust. Possibly it had been there for years, unnoticed. It was crammed with all sorts of drawings. More Picassos, of course.

"Wow!" I mused, as I got ready to pounce in case Louis should think the drawings were scrap paper (and you know what *that* would have meant). "I wonder what *they* would bring on the open market?" I began to figure their value.

Then I heard a door open and a riotous *"Bon jour!"*

Then there was much backslapping and handshaking from a sun-bronzed man with gray hair, in a hunter's cap, a tweed jacket, corduroy trousers, and a plaid woolen shirt. He had an Indian silk scarf printed in reds and yellows around his neck.

He turned toward Louis and said, *"Eh bien! Voilà le personnage Louis XIV!"* He picked him up, brushed away a curl of dust that had become attached to his tail, then kissed him directly on the nose.

All of this time telephones were ringing, doorbells were jangling, and Jaime Sabartes' voice, like a tambour drum beating out an accompaniment to a stage action, repeated and repeated, *"Picasso est occupé! Picasso est occupé!"* Sounded unfriendly, but I have heard from some of the younger painters that Picasso is most generous with his time. He will always have a moment, if asked, to criti-

[1] Months later I found out I was right about the living doves, for Monsieur Picasso actually has a dovecote on his upper floor, that part of the building that is the sanctum sanctum sanctorum.

cize a painting, and freely gives students his advice on color and technique. They say, too, that he frequently gives his opinions on politics, his enemies, food and wine, and sports cars—and most certainly cats.

He considered Louis's total effect through an improvised view finder which he constructed with his two hands, then he made the most Picassoesque remark I was ever to hear: "Those colors, those proportions, and those cerulean-blue eyes! Exactly what I would have done!"

Jaime Sabartes stood by impatiently for his turn to embrace Louis. Whether it was a lack of courage, or in deference to the *maître*, he observed etiquette and waited for the chance. When he did put his hand out to scratch Louis's ear, Picasso, who knows all about a Siamese cat's nature, called out angrily to him: "Hey! Sabartes! Attention!" His voice was as sharp as if Louis were a coiling cobra about to strike.

Dear, sweet Sabartes, humiliated in front of us by the rebuff, said, "But, Pablo, *you* embraced him."

"That's different," said Picasso, pounding his chest. "I'm *Picasso* and the cat *knows* it."

We laughed, and my husband thought it a good moment to focus his camera.

Picasso saw him and glowered with anger. "No! No!" he shouted. "No pictures!"

We were crestfallen. He amended his position.

"Of me, yes. As many as you want. But with Louis, no! I do not pose with a cat!"

"But you kissed him!" I heard myself saying.

"Yes, I kissed him," said Picasso, "because I *love* him, but I wish no photograph with him. I want them to look at *my* face—not his."

And that's why there's no picture of Louis and Picasso in this book.

CHAPTER SEVENTEEN

More
of
Louis's Friends

There are, you will see, pictures of Louis with many other famous cat lovers. I don't propose to name-drop, but how to avoid it? When you travel with a cat you must take him visiting, and in the nature of my husband's business, we visited mostly people who looked well at the other end of a camera—looked well, and could be sold to *Life, Paris Match, Harper's Bazaar, Jours de France, Das Schoenste, Elegante Weld, Europa.*

So it was that we met Blaise Cendrars.

Monsieur Cendrars, the author of *L'Or, Rhum, Hors la loi,* and *La Vie dangereuse,* lived in a charming old house near Denfert Rochereau, facing the back walls of the Santé Prison. He was a cat man, this great writer, but I'm afraid he was a dog man first. If you know his work, and you should, you will remember many references to his favorite dog, whose name was Wagon-Lit.

I respect *anybody's* taste in pets, no matter how curious, but Wagon-Lit scared the hell out of me. You've never seen a more curious dog: the body of a hound, the legs of a chihuahua, irregularly spotted in brown and black, with an unattractive, belligerent personality. Unattractive certainly to me—and by no means a pen pal to Louis.

The barking and miaowing when they met turned into shrieks of rage and screams of terror. I suggested I'd better take Louis out.

But Monsieur Cendrars would not hear of letting us banish Louis to the car. Instead, he displayed mastery over Wagon-Lit that would do credit to a professional animal trainer. He ordered the dog to ignore Louis, insisted we let Louis free, and simply by the power of his voice quieted the beasts and prevented the two natural enemies from fighting. By the time lunch was over, Louis was curled up next to Wagon-Lit, and my heart had almost stopped pounding—but my digestion was ruined.

It was a divine lunch but I ate nothing. Proving that taking a cat with you may help you to reduce.

I didn't eat much at Lenore Fini's either.

I'd never met her, when we went to photograph her, but *everyone* was talking about her imaginative décors for the ballet and theater, her paintings, and her important place in the history of Dadaism and Surrealism.

What they didn't talk about was Miss Fini's big black cat. He had just become a father and was so proud, self-important, and jealous, he was convinced that Louis was either a lounge lizard or Jack the Ripper.

Our lunch with Miss Fini, despite all our efforts to be civil and darling, was rather like the siege of Sedan. The cats were at war, and we couldn't help but take sides, and we ended up with some good pictures, but we were bade a precipitate and frosty good-by and were never asked again.

Jacques Villon, on the other hand, asked us again—but with the stern admonition never again to bring Louis. As a matter of fact, I admire Monsieur Villon's stern, aristocratic character as much as I do his paintings. The moment he saw that Louis and his cat had no rapport, the one for the other, he ordered Louis off the property forthwith and no appeal to a higher court.

As a result, my husband and I had an excellent lunch, but Louis sulked for three weeks.

I anticipated no such trouble with Jean Cocteau.

Have you ever stopped to consider what Cocteau does—and does better than anyone else? He is like an octopus with eight arms, each one on its own—writing plays and films, directing them, costuming them, creating ballets and poetry and paintings. One part of him is a member of the Académie Française, while another part is president of the Cat Club of France. Cocteau has time to be enchanting and he has time to love cats.

At his Paris studio at Porte de Lilas, he was receiving visitors between rehearsals for an avant-garde ballet pantomime, *Oedipus Rex*, which, with a Stravinsky score, was to be given that season at the Twentieth Century Festival of Arts in Paris. Cocteau had designed the costumes and the settings, had supervised the choreography and, since he had nothing else to do, planned to narrate the legend of Oedipus at all the performances.

He greeted the three of us as though he had waited all his life for this moment—and planted a kiss right on Louis's forehead. I breathed easily. This was to be a genuinely happy visit without incident.

Not at all.

What none of us had counted upon was the extraordinary mass of decapitated heads on the floor behind Monsieur Cocteau. Not only were they decapitated, but they had hair of saffron-yellow raffia, eyes that looked like flash bulbs (later, to my astonishment, I found out they were), olive-green complexions, and gaping mouths full of huge, protruding teeth.

Louis took one look at these monsters, declared war, and finally became hysterical. And, even though Monsieur Cocteau tried to soothe him by explaining that the weird things were only masks for his new production, Louis refused to be buttered up. He was having a vendetta with the Cocteau props.

I tried to calm him down and succeeded mildly in diverting his attention. I was relieved when lunch was served *à la* picnic. I had begun on the marvelous *oeufs en gelée*, when two black velvet horses walked into the studio. Well, they weren't horses exactly. They were human beings in leotards with horses' masks on, and unicorn horns. Apparently these human-horse-unicorns loved cats, because as soon as they entered the room they made a beeline for Louis in an effort to cuddle him and assure him of their esteem.

What Louis did to them and Monsieur Cocteau's costumes resulted in great bloody rents in their tights. If you saw *Oedipus Rex* early that season, you would have noticed that, in addition to Monsieur Cocteau's startling wardrobe, two members of the New York City Ballet Company were additionally outfitted in imported court plaster.

If you saw Alberto Moravia, the Italian novelist, later that summer, you would have found him adorned with *two* bits of court
plaster from the same root cause.

It was an August evening and there we were, about nine of us,
sitting around one of those tiny tables on Rosati's terrace. Moravia
was to my right, and Nino Franchina, the sculptor, was to my left.
There was lightning in the air, and summer thunder, and an op-
pressiveness. It was an ominous evening; we were all in bad dark
moods. I suspected that any one of us would argue at the drop of a
hat, and the drop of a hat turned out to be an American Express
Company charabanc, dumping a night tour of Rome right into our
laps.

Moravia and his friends were unhappy at this intrusion and they
all looked at me hopefully because I was an American. There was
even the suggestion that perhaps I could find a way to make them
leave rather quickly. That angered me out of all proportion to the
situation. I argued shrilly that these tourists had a perfect right to
go wherever they wished in Rome, and that, actually, the American
passion for sight-seeing was an exciting and good thing. I found
myself actually humming "The Star-Spangled Banner."

Then one of the tourists, a charming lady, gloved and hatted,
crisp as starch, saw Louis sitting on the chair next to me and came
over to me. She petted him and murmured experienced baby talk,
and then she told me she was from Hackensack, New Jersey, and I
said that I had some cousins in Hackensack, and, while she didn't
know them well, she *did* know them, and we chatted rather confidentially for a few minutes. Moravia and his friends were polite
but, I sensed, disapproving.

Then the lady wondered if she could take Louis over to meet her
friends, and I demurred. "I'm awfully sorry," I said, "but he doesn't
like to be picked up. It makes him angry."

"Cats," said Moravia politely, "do not get angry."

"Oh yes, they do," said the lady from Hackensack. I'm afraid she
was the argumentative type. "I have the cutest little kitten at home
and you never saw such a temper. Really, it's hair-trigger, and quite
uncontrollable. That cat gets as mad as a March hare!"

Moravia smiled pleasantly.

"Sometimes Louis gets as mad as a March hare," I said.

"A cat," Moravia said patiently to me, "has fear, arrogance, resentment, jealousy, envy, and infinite sexual drive. But he has no anger. And, if you'll forgive me, it is not a subject open to argument."

"I certainly don't want to argue," I said, arguing, "but facts are facts, and I've seen Louis very angry—very angry, indeed."

"Of course you have!" said the Hackensack lady.

"I dislike to sound opinionated," said Moravia, "but I frankly think it is impossible. Cats survive only because of their cleverness and their guile. I have made a study of them. I have eight Siamese cats, and I can assure you, my dear Beulaschka,[1] that they do not get angry."

"Dear me," said the lady from Hackensack, "so nice talking to you. Will you excuse me?" She walked with dignity to the other side of the café.

"Cats do get angry," I said to Moravia.

"I dislike to prove so charming a woman wrong," he said, "but let us make a scientific experiment. Are there some sounds Louis doesn't like?"

"Oh yes," I said, "Vespas, Lambrettas, inflating tires, pneumatic drilling, electric razors, mixers and blenders, the toot of a ship's whistle . . ."

"Snapping fingers?" he asked.

"Oh yes, by all means," I said, "snapping fingers."

"Excellent," he said. "We can now conduct our experiment."

He stood up, went over to Louis, and snapped his fingers in Louis's face seventeen times, like a machine gun.

Louis let out a low sinister growl.

"Not angry," said Moravia, "simply a warning."

"Then be warned," I advised.

He continued snapping his fingers and Louis, as cool as a cucumber, raised his paw and, with malice, deliberately and with premeditation, scratched Moravia's right hand—a long, deep, angry scratch.

Moravia was stunned. A waiter tried to pour a little cognac over the scratch, claiming that cognac was as efficacious as iodine—and there were other suggestions for therapy and first aid. But Moravia pushed them all aside.

"Penicillin!" Mr. Moravia said, almost to himself. "I must have

[1] For a reason absolutely unconnected with the Soviet Union, my Italian friends use the Russian diminutive when they address me.

some penicillin!" And hotfooted it for the first-aid station across the
street on Via di Ripetta.

In all conscience, I started after him, but my other friends at the
table prevailed upon me not to go. They knew that Moravia preferred to be alone when he was wounded.

The lady from Hackensack came over to see what she could do.
"He was quite unwise about your cat," she said sympathetically,
"and provoked him. He was probably not knowledgeable."

"Oh, I'm sorry," I said, "he's extraordinarily knowledgeable. He's
Alberto Moravia, the famous novelist. I don't suppose you've read
any of his books?"

"Oh yes," said the lady from Hackensack. "I've read all of them
—Two Women, Stories of Rome, Woman of Rome—and he knows a
great deal about human beings. That I will admit." And then she
leaned closer and said confidentially, "But men, my dear, men may
know about other men and about women—but let me tell you, no
man knows anything about a cat."

I don't agree with that. I think Carlo Levi, the author of Christ
Stopped at Eboli and The Watch, knows a great deal about cats,
even though he prefers dogs. He came in late one afternoon for a
drink and brought his poodle with him. I knew that poodle's reputation as a battler and I immediately banished Louis into the bedroom, forgetting that Louis's dinner was waiting in the kitchen.

While we were chatting over a vermouth, Carlo Levi's poodle
investigated the kitchen and ate Louis's dinner—and what a dinner
it was, too—lamb kidneys, canned milk, and a dish of Kibbled Dog
Biscuit for dessert—imported, I'll have you know, at the cost of $3.85
for the five-pound box.

It was Levi who saw his dog licking his chops, and who put
two and two together. We went into the kitchen to investigate the
theft.

And then Levi showed how much he knew about cats. "Signora,"
he said, "you will now have trouble with your cat. They will not eat
from a plate from which a dog has eaten—particularly this dog. I
advise that you dispose immediately of the food dish and the water
pan."

"But I have no others," I protested.

"You will," he said, and bowed low, and left.

An hour later there were delivered to me four of the most enchanting Ginori dishes I have ever seen.

And that is why, when you come to my house, you have soup from plates that were Carlo Levi's gift to Louis.

Louis has had other gifts. When you come to dinner you will see that I summon my day's worker with an exquisite little silver bell. Courtesy of Anna Magnani.

When Miss Magnani came to call, with a brassière strap and the edge of her slip showing, Louis looked at her with fascination.

"What's the matter, little cat?" she asked. "You haven't seen womans before?"

She took off her mink coat and dropped it on the floor. "Learn to know woman," she said. "Use my coat for your bed."

But Louis was too overcome to obey her, and he fled into a hall closet.

While my husband was taking Miss Magnani's picture, and she was sipping wine and shelling hazelnuts, Louis decided to have a look at her again. He suddenly jumped on the back of the chair on which she was sitting.

She let out a wild, piercing scream. I grabbed Louis and my husband tried to reassure Miss Magnani.

She apologized. "I love cats," she said. "I love you. I love this house. But I cannot bear to be touched unexpectedly."

The next day she sent us the exquisite silver bell. It was much too good for Louis.

Other women have frightened and been frightened by Louis. Zizi Jeanmaire said of him, "Cats are the most graceful creatures in the world. In order to dance well, one must study the cat."

Suzy Parker said: "Louis has all the grace of a fashion model and he's marvelous to sing to. The moment you're even slightly off key, he raises his whiskers."

Sophia Loren said to Louis: "You know, it's extraordinary, but we look alike."

CHAPTER EIGHTEEN

Still More
of
Louis's Friends

Louis could not have looked *less* like Edith Sitwell.

She came to tea one afternoon with Aldous Huxley to be photographed, and she ignored Louis utterly. That irritated him and he used every seductive wile he knew to make her notice him. But Dame Edith, sitting stiffly on a chair in her massive cape outlined in jet with her great emerald ring,[1] refused to notice him. I'd prepared quite a party for her—Banbury tarts, and shortbread, rocks and crumpets, currant buns and poundcake, and terribly thinly sliced bread with water cress and cucumber. I offered her some.

She shook her head faintly. "I don't *eat* my tea," she said. "I drink it."

Mr. Huxley, to cover this moment, pointed to Louis at her ankle and said, "At least pet him, my dear."

Madam Edith looked at him icily over her teacup. "I don't *pet* my tea," she paraphrased, in high literary style, "I drink it."

On all other subjects but cats, Dame Edith was gracious and polite.

Afro, the best of the Italian non-objective painters, was even gracious and polite when Louis got sick in his studio.

Afro has a passion for neatness. Unlike most of his contempo-

---

[1] Somebody once was deeply impressed with this ring and asked:
   "Trabert & Hoeffer? The Duc de Verdura?"
   "No," said Dame Edith. "Cellini."

raries in Italy and Paris, and even Greenwich Village, his studio is as sterile as a surgery.

Most of the modern abstractionists do not work from tubes of paint; instead they have great gallon cans of everything from enamel to barn paint. There are piles of rubbish and rags, twigs, rusty wire, plaster of Paris—to say nothing of Paris green. Some work with an acetylene torch instead of a brush; others use a broom. I know one Roman who applies soiled rags over plaster, and then sprays the lot. The result looks like a relief map of the Aleutians, sells for quite a lot of money, and makes the studio an incredible mess.

But that is not so with Afro. His colors are arranged in orderly rows. The yellows creep slowly from chrome to the deepest ochre. The reds change from rose into scarlet lake and then burnt sienna. The blues from the color of a baby's eyes to the look of the Mediterranean on a stormy day. The greens from an insipid Nile to the evil viridian of algae. The mauves from the palest violet to the deep purple of royal robes.

That is, they *did*—until we all went to visit Afro at his studio— and Louis, a devout admirer of color,[2] turned the studio into a shambles. In three seconds, while Afro, my husband, and I discussed where best to photograph him, Louis upset a table, broke a bowl, and covered himself and the floor with a kind of do-all adhesive of which Afro is very fond.

And then, to make matters worse, Louis was ill.

A lesser man than Afro would have been, and should have been, angry. But his first thought was of Louis—and he plied him with milk to act as an antidote and soothed him and let him fall asleep in his arms.

Our apologies were hollow. It turned out they were unnecessary. Afro merely smiled and said, "We can easily clean up the studio. What is important is that no living thing be ill or in pain. Take him home and watch him, and tomorrow I will . . ." He hesitated.

We waited breathlessly for what he would do tomorrow.

"And tomorrow I will try somehow to find his color in all these paints. If I do, I'll send you the picture."

I don't think he ever managed to capture Louis on canvas; he sent us another picture.

[2] There are those who say cats are color blind. I do *not* agree. They may see only gray, but at least they're different grays with their own vibrations.

So did Di Chirico.

Di Chirico, for half a century, has meant unlikely pink horses running rampant through unending arches, sky-piercing smoke-stacks, and points that actually vanish three miles from where they start. His pictures are highly valued. Unfortunately, Di Chirico hates them. He hates his pink horses, his cube on cube. He detests his endless arches and his vanishing points. He has endless arguments with himself about his new theories and his old.

But about cats he is as old-fashioned as Whistler's mother.

The day we went to photograph him, Louis was talkative and ugly, making grunting and moaning sounds and refusing to shut up. Di Chirico said he had the answer.

He sent his housekeeper for some butter and then spread it on Louis's forepaws. Louis had to get it off and he was so busy licking away that he stopped his chatter.

Di Chirico was prouder of his knowledge of cats than of any of his pink horses.

Di Chirico does not know how he saved us from dreadful embarrassment with Stravinsky.

We went to photograph the maestro one day while he was in rehearsal at the Philharmonic Auditorium in Los Angeles. He had particularly asked that we bring Louis along. He kissed my hand and patted Louis expertly, and then he asked whether Louis had ever heard his *"Berceuse des Chats."*

We sadly admitted that he had not, and then Stravinsky pulled together a few of his violinists and flutists and played a version of it just for Louis.

Unfortunately, it offended Louis's sensitive eardrums, and he started to make terrible noises.

I looked around quickly, saw that a musician had left a half-eaten ham sandwich on a paper plate. I grabbed it, took off the butter, and put it on Louis's forepaws. Louis stopped squawking and appeared to enjoy the concert to his honor.

Stravinsky never knew.

When Cary Grant heard the story about Louis and Stravinsky, he laughed, and then he looked a little solemn. I was eating an ice cream cone and letting Louis have some. Mr. Grant did not approve. He, as you may or may not know, is a devotee of health foods—prefers carrots to chocolate and, of course, polyunsaturated fats to butter.

He smiled his famous smile and pointed at Louis. "You see," he said, "this beautiful creature is an example of a high protein diet. That sleek coat, those brilliant eyes, his muscle tone, his agelessness are tributes to proper eating. We'd do well to follow his example, because we're all committing suicide with our diets."

Aldous Huxley agrees with Mr. Grant about diet and about the usefulness of many other forms of natural herbs.

When next we saw him, he told us how sorry he was about Edith Sitwell's inattention to Louis. While he did not agree that all people who dislike cats are villains, he did feel that they were denying themselves some of the pleasures of life, and modestly said that he had once written an essay called *Sermons in Cats*. I was embarrassed to admit I'd never read it.

He was gracious enough to send it to me and only lately I called him and asked him if I might quote two paragraphs. He agreed readily.

"Observe," he advises, "a pair of Siamese cats, and you will see civilized man without the lid of convention, manners and traditions of thought and feeling, beneath which each of us passes his or her existence."

And later, in continuing to talk of the Siamese, he says: "They are, if not the most beautiful, certainly the most striking and fantastic, for what disquieting blue eyes stare from the black velvet mask of their faces. Their forepaws are gloved almost to the shoulder like the long black kid arms of Yvette Guilbert. Over their hind legs are tightly drawn the black silk stockings with which Felicien Rops so perversely and indecently clothed his nudes. . . . Their tails are tapering black serpents, endowed, even when the body lies in Sphynx-like repose, with a spasmodic and uneasy life of their own. And what strange voices they have. Sometimes like the complaining of small children, sometimes like the noises of lambs, sometimes like the agonized and furious howling of lost souls. Compared with these fantastic creatures, other cats, however beautiful and engaging, are apt to seem a little insipid."

That's what the man said.

All men are not Aldous Huxley. Some even dislike cats intensely —and I do mean Georges Braque.

That day came when, on assignment, we went to Varangeville to photograph him. I instinctively wanted Louis to stay at home, but the rendezvous with Braque coincided with the *grand nettoyage mensuel*[1] of our room at the Lutèce. This monthly (sic) general cleaning, *entre nous*, was so irregular that often I toyed with the idea that French months must have at least ninety days instead of thirty. The cleaning was an all-day affair, God knows, with three months' worth of dust, dirt, lazy drains, hollowed mattresses, spiderwebs, bathtub rings, and dirty windows to be removed in those few short hours between after breakfast and before supper.

One of the *femmes de chambre* objected to Louis watching her work. (She was the one who kept the white mouse.) "He acts just like the *Ministre de Travail!*"

It wasn't that I didn't trust her, but anyone who keeps a white mouse because he might be a bewitched prince might just use a *plastique* on a cat because he reminds her of the Minister of Labor. Too, I didn't want her mind to be on revolution. I preferred her concentration on the dust under the beds.

At that time we were the proud owners of a Citroën which we called Sam the CitroAm. Sam was exactly like a Frenchman. He had a mind of his own, and an engine unlike any of the other fifty million Citroëns which the fictional fifty million Frenchmen drive.

We started just after dawn for Varangeville on the Normandy coast. That day the rain was falling as only it can fall in Paris in the early spring—a thin fine spray more like the discharge of an atomizer. Sam the CitroAm had been parked on the street all night. By morning his sparkplugs were water-soaked, his transmission soggy, and his well-advertised front-wheel drive an empty joke. Without Sam, our appointment with Braque was impossible to keep. One does not take a taxi to Varangeville. Nor does one take the train, which doesn't even stop there.

Louis and I sat in Sam, our worthless, good-for-nothing Sam, while my husband went to look for a mechanic in an all-night garage. An hour later my husband, the mechanic, and an unusual-looking truck pulled up to the Lutèce. Some sort of wire was attached to a coil under the bonnet, then an exchange of Gauloise cigarettes, a wait of ten minutes, and Sam began to chug.

[1] Grand cleaning monthly.

We were off to Varangeville, but there was no way to notify Monsieur Braque that we were an hour late. We had carelessly forgotten to ask for his telephone number, and anyone knows that a telegram, in France, arrives long after the emergency is over.

As we rowed our way out of Paris, my husband began his usual check-off: did we have the cameras, the box of photographs, Louis, the sandbox, the address? No, we didn't have the address. Rather, I had forgotten my little blue book, but anyone who was anybody in Varangeville would *know* Monsieur Braque. How many illustrious citizens could there be in a town of fifteen hundred people? And how many named Braque?

Sam the Citroën, with a mind of its own, splashed through the puddles on the highway. His windshield wiper seemed to moan, "*Je veux chez moi, je veux chez moi* [I want to go home. I want to go home]." The route was long and complicated, but we did come to Dieppe just before noon. Now I was to be my husband's badly paid assistant by asking the way to Braque's house. A rainy day in Dieppe is not anybody's idea of *grand confort*,[2] so most of the Dieppiens were fortifying themselves with calvados in places a little drier than the main street. It took more than twenty minutes to find anyone in Dieppe who would even admit he had ever heard of Varangeville. Finally, one old woman admitted (fortified against the weather by home-brewed calvados) that she was born there. Varangeville was only a few kilometers from Dieppe, but it might have been in Arkansas.

It was Apple Blossom Time in Normandy, and the orchard in which Georges Braque's house stands looked like the decorations for a bridal shower. No bride was I, though, in my soggy Burberry and wilted hair, as we drove up in front of Monsieur Braque's house and I tried to find the bell. No bell. So I knocked, breaking two nails. I swore some good old Brooklyn oaths.

No wonder Monsieur Braque stared at me with horror when he came to the door. He did not have to explain that he was at lunch, for his napkin was still around his neck, and he held a fork in his right hand, with the remains of a succulent Normandy *ragoût* clinging to its tines. From my husband's point of view, my encounter with Braque must have looked like a silent movie. We both talked with our hands, mine continually pointing in the direction of Paris

2 Grand comfort.

—his pointing to his wristwatch. Then I pointed to the car; he pointed to the interior of his cottage. I assumed he wished us to enter, though it was hard to tell.

Self-consciously, we went in, and stood in little puddles, and all my French deserted me, but Braque rose to the occasion by using extremely vivid sign language, and his housekeeper took our coats, and bade us to his table.

Polite he was; happy to see us he wasn't. Who could blame him? We were five hours late; we had totally upset his busy schedule. Under the circumstances, he was far more gracious than I would have been. As for Louis, he took a peek at him, murmured (as I've already told you), "What a coincidence. Braque colors," and refused to let him stay in the house. Outside went Louis to the car, and I was miserable. Braque was occupied with his next course: boiled beef.

We had a soggy and silent lunch. When he finished his final course, cheese and fruit, he agreed to sit for my husband, and the business of photography was carried out in silent bad temper.

"Are these color pictures?" he asked. My husband nodded.

"Then I demand the cat," said Braque.

Go figure it.

Picasso, who loved cats, refused to be photographed with one.

Braque, who loathed them, insisted on it.

His explanation was meager, but apparently he thought Louis set him off. Or perhaps his great sense of composition told him that Louis would help make better pictures. I don't really know. That's what Monsieur Braque wanted.

And what Braque wants, Braque gets.

CHAPTER NINETEEN

The
Cat Haters

When we got back to Paris, I stayed in bed for two days with vertigo, headache, and Ménière's syndrome, also tonsillitis.

And, in bed, I considered many matters, chiefly Louis. I reviewed his virtues and his faults, and *my* virtues and *my* faults, and I had to face facts ruthlessly. Louis was not exactly a darling, nor was I, foisting him on people.

You see, love is not blind. At least I hope my love for Louis is not. I observed Louis from the point of view of the opposition, the cat hater, or the cat tolerator. Detach yourself from all sentiment and what do you see? A hedonist, a pleasure-bent, selfish beast, a mixture of love and hate, pride and humility, grace and ingratitude. When I really face the issue, I say, in the words Molnar used to describe Hungarians,[1] "If you have a cat for a friend, you don't need an enemy." I face the issue, often.

I stare right at Louis and say, "You are a fiend, darling, an absolute atavistic beast. You scratch and claw, you bite the hand that feeds you, you shed, you know too much, you're moody and inconsistent, and at times you're about as sentimental as a lion. And what a bother you are."

No wonder so many people are anti-cat. I've met many of them and they logically divide into several well-defined categories:

1. *The Cat Haters.*

Some of my friends really and truly have a morbid loathing of cats. I heard a lady remark once about their "snakelike heads."

[1] Which some of my best friends are.

She was absolutely revolted by my living with one of *them*, and the sight of my kissing Louis drove her, raving, into the night.

2. *The Nervous.*

These just are edgy with cats. My mother, for instance, a wild West Highland White lover, doesn't trust Louis—a trauma that dates back to her childhood when a kitten scratched her. The kitten was small. *She* was small, but the intense fright of that moment never left her.

3. *The Allergy People.*

Those who *claim* to have a negative reaction to cat dander (whatever that is). It used to be totally embarrassing to me when a guest suddenly swelled after dinner, or sneezed incessantly after passing my threshold. All of this happened *after* they knew I had a cat, never before.

4. *The Craig's Wives.*

The too particular housekeeper who cannot relinquish the sanctity of her parlor to cat hairs and scratched furniture. A cat isn't sanitary enough for *her*—if she only *knew* how clean he really is!

5. *The He-Man.*

"Cats are for sissies and old maids," says he.

6. *The Selfish Ones.*

They will not give one moment of their spare time to caring for anyone but themselves. "I want to be *free!* I want to come and go as I like!"

7. *The Brain-Washed.*

This group believes cats are vicious, impossible to train, and eat sleeping people. They are victims of years of systematized anti-cat propaganda.

8. *The Tolerant Ones.*

They really dislike cats, but, upon provocation, will say of Louis, "He's just like a dog." I find this patronizing attitude the most intolerable of all.

9. *The Superstitious.*

This jolly collection adds cats to walking under ladders, three on a match, hats on beds, and open umbrellas in a house.

According to a piece in the New York *Times* of July 29, 1962,[2] it began as long ago as the time of the Norse goddess Freyia, who was supposed to preside over evil orgies. Her chariot "was believed

[2] Copyright by the New York *Times.* Reprinted by permission.

to be drawn by two black cats. Cats were considered evil and in many places full dress trials were held for cats on charges of sorcery.

"Throughout France it was once believed that a cat could never suffer enough because it represented the devil. In the Vosges cats were burned on Shrove Tuesday. In Alsace, they were thrown in the Easter bonfire. Sometimes they were hung over the fire from the end of a pole and roasted alive. Shepherds would force their flocks to leap over the fire believing this made them immune to disease and witchcraft.

"In the midsummer bonfire which once burned on the Place de Grève in Paris, a basket or sack of cats was hung from a tall mast in the bonfire. The spectators collected the ashes and took them home for luck.

"Cats have been symbols of luck—or bad luck—in many countries. Seamen believe black cats bring foul weather, but tortoise-shell cats are lucky. In some parts of the Far East cats are sent up the mastheads to chase away the storm devils.

"The Chinese believed that a cat was a cross between a lioness and a monkey. They also thought one could tell the time accurately by a cat's eyes.

"In England it is sometimes said that frost will come when a cat turns its tail to the fire. If it licks the tail, there will be rain.

"Slavs used to burn a blind cat before going to market. They would throw a pinch of its ashes over the person with whom they were bargaining, believing that this would make him as blind as the cat.

"To make rain in Java one has only to bathe a cat. In Europe walling up a cat in a new home will bring luck to the occupants."

Well, while I can't hold with walling up cats, I cannot deny that all of these antipathetic people have something to complain about. And, in rigid self-examination, I've a few complaints myself.

I, for instance, once believed some long-forgotten fashion editor who made the following statement: "You're always well dressed in beige." Am I now? I'm one of the world's worst-dressed women, and it's all Louis's fault.

I've hypnotized myself into thinking I look well in it but *really, really,* I don't! Camel's hair, taupe, kasha cloth, oatmeal tweed, and natural cashmere bring out the yellows in my skin, emphasize my graying hair, and accentuate my hipline. Besides, it can be damned boring.

I yearn for one of those little nothings of a black dress. I covet a black velvet to wear with pearls. I envy those simple little navy-blue Chanels, those marvelous black turtlenecks, the Oxford-gray flannels. It isn't that I don't look *well* in these inky colors. On the contrary, my skin loses all of its sallowness, nobody seems to notice my gray hair, and my hips diminish to such a proportion that at times I don't know myself. Look *well?* I look *divine* in black, but Louis looks terrible *on* it!

My wardrobe, since I've had Louis, is like the inside and outside of a mushroom. Louis is like that too. This truffle camouflage of mine is not an obsession. It is a convenience.

My collection of clothesbrushes would make even the Smithsonian Institution salivate with envy. Boar bristle? I have it. Porcupine quill? I have it. Sticky-tape mitts? I have ten. Magnetized something or other? I have that. Special attachments on my vacuum cleaner? Yes, sir! Like a witch, I even use a broom to tidy up the four-yard circle of my navy-blue flannel Moroccan burnoose. I don't wear it often, but it looks so well at an opening that I patiently give three hours of my precious time to sweep it clean.[3]

Gentlemen who own Siamese cats also have a pretty tough time. My husband had a blue flannel Hawes and Curtis blazer, which attracted cat hairs like a magnet. He wrote me once from the Belgian Congo to tell me that although Louis was 17,895 miles from him, and hadn't been closer in three months, he still found his hairs clinging to the cloth. Fortunately, Sandy was a very sentimental man where cats were concerned and he never insisted that we exchange Louis for a navy-blue one.

When you have a Siamese around the house or clothes closet, we both learned that certain fabrics are safe, others are half safe, and the rest belong in that dream world that other people inhabit. Not *you!* Some prints with a lot of beige in them do beautifully. Polka dots or navy or black, *never.* Black jersey is the *absolute never.* Black velvet, the *absolute never never.* A gentleman's dinner jacket? Oh dear, it's such a necessity, too!

Brushing a cat helps. It removes a good deal of the excess hair from the cat and you have great wads of silky, beige fiber. Just

[3] To remove cat hairs, the only thing that *really* works is infinite concentration and a pair of tweezers.

great if you spin. There's a lady in Finland whose two chow dogs produce so much fluff that she had four pillow cases full of their combings before a year was out. She bought a spinning wheel, worked the distaff and spindle, and came away with a yarn that was softer, fuzzier, and certainly much rarer than vicuña. Then, with a diligence only to be matched by her medieval cousins, who spun hair shirts, she knitted, crocheted, and wove the unusual strands into cardigans, jumpers, and tweeds.

Siamese cats produce the same quality of fluff, which although not as abundant as that of a chow is ersatz vicuña. I actually bid on and captured a spinning wheel at an auction, but unfortunately some essential parts were missing and my enthusiasm was dampened.[4] The darned thing looked too folksy with my Directoire chairs and absolutely non sequitur with the Venetian chest. I scrapped the entire idea of turning my house into a cottage industry. Anyway, who needs a cashmere sweater? Beige—yet!

Oh yes, cashmere? Dan Taradash, the screen writer, and his wife Madeleine have a Siamese cat with the most eccentric habit. It eats cashmere sweaters with the passion of a moth. When it can't find cashmere it will settle for camel's-hair coats, flannel suits, oriental rugs, or Hudson Bay blankets. If it's wool, it's delicious! His appetite is insatiable, and he won't take liver for an answer.

Wool eating in Siamese is not uncommon. My lithographer friend June Wayne had one who actually ate the sleeve off her coat as she was watching a television program. The trouble with that was she hadn't even decided to buy it. It still bore the Saks Fifth Avenue price tag of $175 when she gave it to the Salvation Army.

I must make a confession. Louis *used* to have that monkey on his back. It lasted for about two years and then he either joined WEA (Wool Eaters Anonymous) or simply outgrew it. His *passion de laine* almost cost my husband his career in the early days when he first took to photography for a living. After many lean months, he finally was commissioned by the wife of a Pasadena stockbroker to do her portrait.

Mrs. F—— arrived at our apartment wearing the most glorious set of pistachio-green cashmere sweaters I had ever seen. (The *full* Burlington Arcade—not a shilling less than twenty pounds.) She had not planned to be photographed in them, so she brought

4 I gave it to a friend who planted it with philodendron.

along a little black dress with a wide décolletage for the sitting.

In those days we had no dressing room for our subjects, so she changed in our bedroom, leaving her valuable woolies on the bed. *Doomsday!*

I was so busy helping my husband, I never let a thought drift to Louis. I assumed he was asleep somewhere, but was I wrong! During the forty-five minutes of the sitting and the fifteen minutes for tea, Louis ate and digested one cuff, one sleeve, one lower back, and one upper front of the pistachio cashmeres. When I saw him, he was licking his chops and washing his front paws. He was altogether disgusting in his complacency about his gluttony.

Mrs. F—— was charming about her loss; she was insured. The adjuster called me to check her story, and came over in person to investigate. He was skeptical, until Louis ate the collar of his overcoat. Oh, not ate, just a few threads—but Mrs. F—— got her check.

I did not take this matter lying down. I consulted my vet, who told me in a funeral-parlor voice that any sort of morbid appetite in a cat or dog is a warning of a vitamin or calcium deficiency. I'm sure this is scientifically true, but I also think that Siamese cats just *love* wool. Maybe it's the taste, maybe the texture, maybe the lanolin. Whatever it *is*, they need a fix once in a while. Cod-liver oil, brewer's yeast, and vitamin A never seem to taste as yummy.

I have some advice to the owners of wool eaters: you either get rid of your cat or change to orlon.

And that applies to furniture as well. Furniture! I think I've already mentioned that it takes a house cat at least six months to tatter the arm of a chair, but that depends, too, on the fabric. Toile de Jouy would die a horrible death in a month; Peruvian linen lasts a little longer; satins and brocade ten days and two hours. Nubby fabrics won't show the damage for a long time and velveteen is surprisingly sturdy, although its tenacious habit of holding onto cat hairs makes it impractical. Kittens' claws take a terrible toll in nylon curtains and point d'esprit net. The only answer is a fabric made of genuine "mother of plastic," which I don't mind for outdoor furniture. When I saw Louis valiantly and hopelessly trying to rip a very contemporary chair, a bit of verse came into my head:

> *Blessings on you, Naugahyde,*
> *We can't scratch through,*
> *I know, I tried!*

Still, you can't change your nature. I'm for silks and satins, chintzes and linens, hand-woven woolens, and watered taffetas, as much as the next one. I hate the ersatz, but fabric chemists, or whatever you call them, have come up with some divine ersatz moirés which might have fooled even Elsie de Wolfe. It's a catproof cat trap that lets them claw to infinity without even denting its surface. Comes in divine colors, too, made for Regency sofas and bergère chairs, and not the least of its virtues is that you can do your housekeeping with a hose.

If you prefer not to use synthetics (and who can blame you?) the only way you can save your furniture is to try to get your cat to scratch something else. Because scratch he will. So get a scratching post.

There are, you will find, as many varieties of scratching posts as cats. I'm sorry to report that *none of them works*—that is, not for long! A carpeted two-by-four post with catnip underneath has a certain fascination until the catnip loses its freshness and flavor. Another problem is that the post falls down unless securely anchored, and thus frustrates a cat who likes to scratch standing up. Result: he ignores the pole and goes to work on your chaise.

At a cat show in London recently, a young man displayed what he called "the most infallible scratching post in the world with a money-back guarantee." It was nothing but a pine log, ten inches in diameter and twenty-four in length. His demonstration at the show was done without cats, but the thoroughly ripped, shaggy remains of a once proud log testified to his claim. A log ought to serve well—but there are few houses in which a log looks really well.

Certainly not in the *cabinet particulier* of Raymond and Barbara Grosset in Paris. They moon over their cats, but they also are passionate about their Aubusson chairs and their seventeenth-century *boiserie*. They found the answer: a few sheets of cork were added to the dado in their sitting room—painted pale gray like the rest of the wall. They hang amusingly, if you like that sort of thing, from red velvet ribbons; in point of fact, they are firmly nailed to the walls at respectable intervals at cat height. The cats use them constantly, which, however, does *not* stop the curious visitor from asking, "What are *those* for?"

I have not indulged in this kind of protective carpentry—or taken any other steps against Louis's claws. Nor have I disciplined him when I caught him on a newly upholstered chair. At worst, I may have uttered a sotto voce *"Scat!"* but I guess it just isn't in my blood to kick him in the rear or throw a paperback at him—a method strongly recommended by a gentleman cat breeder. He would call me an unsuitable cat owner, I suppose, but this *chat gâté* (spoiled cat) of mine is my problem—and I've no intention of knocking his brains out because he does what comes naturally. I try to deal with the matter rationally, from the cat's point of view.

You can observe a cat scratching for years and never quite make up your mind about the *raison d'être*. Sometimes they do it because they are *mad*[5]—they use it as a sort of release for their aggressions. At other times they derive great pleasure and satisfaction from the stretching exercise. (I'm also convinced that spite enters into it somewhere, but *where* I'll never know.)

The most acceptable theory about clawing is simple—cats have to get rid of the outer sheath of their nails. Their clawing is simply their way of giving themselves a manicure. So *you* do it.

Put on your white dress, get your files and emery boards, and little basin, and give your cat a manicure yourself. No cuticle pushing and no polish, remember. Just snip the points off his front claws with a toenail clipper. It blunts them for about ten days, then they grow back.

During the growing period, I've seen Louis try to hone a point on them again, and I have *news* for you—he uses the furniture! But the damage is less severe. And he's only doing what his ancestors did in the jungle a hundred thousand years ago.

For a cat has claws as a rose has thorns. All members of the Felidae family have retractable ones, except the cheetah. (His stay out all the time—because life is tough in the jungles of Ceylon and nature has given him the weapons to be a pretty tough cookie.)

And nails aren't all of it. Let's not forget teeth. The bite of a teething kitten is one thing. The bite of a grown cat, another. Confession: I've already admitted that Louis, my dear friend and darling enemy, once bit my hand. That "once" is a lie. Often is a better word.

But there were reasons—cat reasons, of course, and if you think like a cat, you'll agree that he was right. The serious bites were not those given in play, where my hand was the mouse. Or, in a little vaudeville routine, when Louis, imagining himself as a bur-

[5] Ho! Ho! Moravia!

lesque comic, will nip at my nose when I'm not looking. No! He meant to bite and he did, quite thoroughly.

For instance, one late afternoon of a summer day, when the scorching sun had set behind the Beverly Hills City Hall, I took Louis out for a walk. It wasn't really a walk, just a stroll into our garden for some fresh (un-air-conditioned) air. Suddenly the hackles began to rise on his back and an ugly sound came from his throat. His personality changed completely. In a few minutes I knew why: another cat, an intruder, was on his property.[6] I *thought* I knew *all* about cats, so *this* smart-aleck reached down to quiet her emotionally disturbed pussy cat.

I blacked out and awakened in the Beverly Hills Emergency Hospital with a doctor stitching a fine seam in my wrist, and his assistant coaxing tetanus antitoxin and penicillin into my unwilling veins. They seemed to be quite experienced in this sort of mending, admitting that almost every day somebody (usually the human *third party*) gets his come-uppance as a result of trying to separate two cats.

"Let them kill each other," advised the cynical physician, "keep out of their business."

I went home and called up my vet. I had to talk to *somebody* sympathetic.

"How can it be that Louis would attack me?" I asked. "Me—whom he loves. Me, who loves him. Me. The love object."

"At the moment, you're not the love object," said the vet. "You're a threat. You're another cat. You're attacking from the rear. His concentration to survive is so great that anything or anybody that touches him is a mortal enemy. It's pure atavism."

"What do I do if it happens again?"

"Watch out for those back-yard brief encounters," the vet warned. "It may be sex at first sight, or it may be a wiseacre bully who thinks he can call your cat a sissy because he's on a leash. You'll never know how wild a Siamese can be until you see him in action. *But*—let him get the other cat—*not you.* Let go of the leash, run for the nearest entrance, close your eyes and your ears, have a cup of tea, and hope for the best. The atavism finally wears off!"

To be atavistically bitten and clawed by your own cat is some-

---

[6] I once planted catnip in my back yard, and I've lived to regret it. I've poured kerosene on the plants, but nothing will kill them permanently.

thing not even your closest relative will understand. "You're keeping him?" my brother asked incredulously.

I nodded.

"You're a nut!"

"I love him."

"He obviously doesn't love you. Get rid of him."

"I want no advice. You obviously refuse to understand that this is throwback behavior not likely to occur again unless the identical circumstances are repeated."

"Sounds like psychoanalysis."

"Why not?"

"Why *not?*"

I knew I had him, and I couldn't help but go on with it. "Cats can be just as maladjusted as any other living thing. And the science of the mind and behavior applies to them as well as to people."

"Cats are instinctive and do not have reason."

I humphed. "That's all you know about it. I've been thinking for a long time that Louis is neurotic."

"Not neurotic. Just spoiled."

"Would you say that about a child? I think he's traveled too far and he hasn't laid down any roots."

"He certainly tried to lay down some roots on the back of your hand. You may be scarred for life."

"I heal quickly, and I think his action was symptomatic. I may have him take some treatments."

"What kind of treatments?"

"From an analyst."

"What kind of an analyst?"

"A cat analyst."

"Do you mean to tell me there are actually cat analysts?"

"Certainly. And dog analysts, and bird analysts. There's a particularly good cat analyst in Salt Lake City—but I don't think I can afford to have him come here for consulation."

"You are an idiot!"

He stormed out of the house, but sent me a sheaf of yellow roses, and to this day he's not quite sure whether I was serious or not about the cat analyst in Salt Lake. I wasn't. There is no such thing.

I wish there were.

CHAPTER TWENTY

The
Cat
Fools

If there were cat analysts, I should think they'd be very busy —not with the animals but with the owners. I assume that you need no further proof that I'm mad for cats and that I go far beyond ordinary limits to please them and make them comfortable. I am not unaware that many of you may even think that I've gone too far.

That's because you don't know how much further there is to go. If you think that I'm a cat lover, kindly remember that I have only *one* cat. It seems to me that I show remarkable reserve.

To fall asleep with a hundred cats on my bed is my secret wish now, as it has been since I was three. But it shall remain only a wish. I don't have the fortitude of Pamela Mason, who houses nearly thirty, not all of them hers. It has been said that a foundling cat left on the Mason doorstep in a basket will be raised with no questions asked. A few years ago we were invited to tea to talk about a reportage my husband was to do for a national magazine on the Masons and their cats. At the stroke of four I heard a gong and a lovely London voice a bit of Hampstead Heath in its pitch, call: "Tea, anyone?" Again, "Tea is ready!"

I, for one, didn't need that much urging, but the invitation was *not* for us. Then, as though by some prearranged rendezvous, the cats came running from all parts of the estate: black ones, gray ones, shaggy ones and smooth ones, Siamese and Persian, short-tailed and no-tailed, young and silly ones, tired matriarchs and youthful patriarchs. A quantity of glass bowls were arranged in a circle, quite a great quantity, for there were a great quantity of cats. Each one stood beside his individual dish and, with the patience of those who know where their next meal is coming from, waited until his ration was served. That day their "tea" was poached sole. It takes quite a lot of time to fillet ten pounds of sole, and quite a lot of money too. But that's *not* why I have only one.

One cat at a time and he's *yours.* Two cats at a time, they belong to *each other.* More than two will bring sibling trouble. More than five, and you might as well change your profession from whatever it is to zookeeper, sandbox changer, kidney cutter, referee, and impartial chairman. How can you hold back favoritism and divide your love equally among twenty-five cats?

There is an irresistible urge to confuse a cat lover with a cat collector. I suppose if you are a *felinophile enragée,* as I am, you should be surrounded by cats. But a barnful doesn't always imply a grand passion. Monogamous me, I love them all, but I want to live with only one.

To be a minority of one among a swarm of cats has been the choice of many great literary men (and women). Colette had a harem; Hemingway an army; Paul Leautaud a tribe; François Coppée a colony with its own private physician.

Stéphane Mallarmé, the French poet, who rather overdid it by living with a dynasty of cats, claimed that cats were necessary adjuncts to a house: they polish furniture, soften the angles, add an air of mystery, and serve as most decorative bibelots.

I agree with Mr. Carl Van Vechten that a cat with its sedative powers is the perfect companion for the writer. One cat, that is! I enjoy Louis immensely when he sits on my lap as I work at my typewriter. I even allow him to paw my papers and play hide-and-go-seek under my carbon paper. His dignity homogenizes with my irritability, makes us a loving couple, and couple we shall remain.

In the world of cat lovers that singleness of purpose means I am a rank amateur. I reluctantly admit that some of the cat fools I've met in the world of cat lovers sometimes tempt me to join the opposition.

For instance, there is a prominent professor at a European university who is working on the theory that history has been changed by cats—that is, he is researching the proposition that the major villains and dictators throughout the ages have been cat haters. He will give you chapter and verse that Napoleon hated cats; he has ample evidence to prove that Hitler hated them even more. He has his staff working on the negative cat attitudes of Mussolini, Tojo, the Kaiser, Benedict Arnold, Aaron Burr, Torquemada, Cesare Borgia (and all the relatives), and Judas Iscariot. Oh yes, and Rasputin.[1]

No, no, I'm not making this up. I'm perfectly serious. That is the professor's research project—and nothing will stop him. Personally, I think he's ripe for the men in white suits.

I have another friend who, while completely sane on every other subject, has absolutely lost her marbles about astrology—not just plain ordinary astrology for you and me but astrology for cats. When I decided to take Louis on another trip, she warned me not to do it without having Louis's horoscope read. I tried to change the subject, but she wouldn't have it. Her argument was that if the lives and destinies of human beings were controlled by the stars, why shouldn't the lives of cats be equally controlled? I could not debate the point, nor did I wish to.

In any case, the next day she sent me Louis's horoscope. It is mimeographed on a sheet of pink paper with whimsical Disney-like characters surrounding it. It appears that Louis is Taurus, as is anybody who is born between April 20 through May 20, and he has many characteristics of which I had never heard before.

For instance, according to his horoscope, he's more than usually affectionate, happy, and intelligent—with an inordinate ability to distinguish between people who love cats and those who do not. It says he's faithful and obedient, and that he'd win prizes in a cat show. It also suggests that if he's to find a wife she should be Scorpio. (I couldn't expect the astrologist to know Louis's secret shame.)

As for his good times of year, January is his best month. February and March, almost anything can happen. In April he's a darling and loves me. In May and June he's sullen and introspective. It is suggested that I cater to his every whim. July, August, and September are splendid for kitten-making and for competition. (I can't

[1] Aline Mosby, who used to be UPI correspondent in Moscow, tells me she's heard a rumor the Khrushchevs keep a cat. I bet my anthropologist friend will find out it belongs to Mrs. Khrushchev.

15.

One of the sights at the Colosseum.

16.

Louis in Rome...

17.

...and exploring the ancient columns.

18.

...with an Italian admirer, Anna Magnani...

imagine what kind.) October, November, and December are his travel months.

The astrologist underlined this last fact. She couldn't have been happier.

I couldn't have been more depressed.

That depression was nothing compared to the day in Paris when Louis had a slight catarrh and I thought I'd better get him a sweater.

Now getting a sweater for a cat is not as idiotic as it might seem; it's pure sense to try to protect him against the cold weather. I visited the Galeries Lafayette and Au Printemps, but there were no cat sweaters; finally a saleslady suggested that I try a shop that specialized in these matters. (I was in Paris again recently and I note that the shop has gone out of business, à cause de the French equivalent of bankruptcy, so there's no point telling you its name.)

But I went there—off the Place Vendôme—in order to get a simple cold-resistant sweater (dun-colored wool, V-neck, cap sleeves). I could tell from the window display that the shop catered not only to cats but to dogs and parakeets and marmosets as well. There was a model of a monkey in a sort of revealing bikini, and that should have warned me, but it didn't, and I went in.

I was greeted effusively by the saleslady wearing the Paris vendeuse uniform, a basic black dress, pearl earrings, and the most amiable of manners. She was holding an atomizer, which she waved at me.

"Bon jour, madame, how about a sample of our new eau de cologne made exclusively for dogs, Chien de Paris?"

"Lovely," I said, "but I have a cat."

"Oui, it's a little overwhelming for cats, but we have Mon Amour, Mon Chat, with a muguet base which they adore." She reached for another atomizer. "This is our newest scent for cats of an oriental breed. Yours is of oriental breed?"

With some nausea, I allowed he was.

"It has a musk base which goes with Siamese and Burmese so well. See, madame?"

I saw.

And she saw I didn't like it. So she picked up another atomizer, pressed the bulb, and anesthetized me, as she murmured: "Chat d'Arabie."

In my chloroformed state, I bought some of it, not for Louis, of course, but for myself, because I can never resist sandalwood or a seductive name like Chat d'Arabie. Whatever Chat d'Arabie contained beside sandalwood remains an unsolvable mystery. Frankly, my nose detected tap water, bay rum, vanilla, and, I think, that paralyzing root so popular in Mexico.

The perfume gambit over, I asked to see sweaters. Madame was not yet ready to come to the point. She had a few other things to sell first.

"Here is a divine little *tablier*. How you call it in English?"

"It's either an apron for a terribly small child," I said, "or a bib."

"Bib?"

I pantomimed—and she was all smiles. "Yes, a beeb," she said, "but not an ordinary one. Real valenciennes lace, madame, and plastic linen. Just tie it around your cat's neck while he eats."

"No, thank you," I said. "Now about your sweaters . . ."

"First," she insisted, "have a look at our mother and litter sets, all matching. *Mignon*, eh?"

I didn't think so.

Then she produced a yellow slicker. "Does your cat go out in the rain? Here's a mackintosh. And to go with it, little overshoes. They're new, madame, sort of an amusing copy of dog shoes."

Repulsive!

I noticed a rack of doll clothes. Or rather, I *assumed* they were doll clothes: party dresses of bonbon-pink mousseline de soie, velvet capes, plumed bonnets.

"Enchanting, are they not, madame?"

"For dolls?"

"For cats, of course, madame, or smallish monkeys, or rabbits. But I think they would look foolish on rabbits."

"Madame," I asked, "*who* would put a cat or a monkey or a rabbit into a dress?"

She looked at me as though my ignorance was showing beyond the hem of my skirt. "But, madame, *everybody* does!"

With that, I asked to see the works. And she showed me the gems of her stock. First, the cat dresses and suits, designed obviously by somebody who used to be with Chanel, since most of them had long waistlines. Then we went on to the boutique items: cat *châteaux*; electrically heated, mauve satin cushions; eighteen-carat gold chains with engraved lockets; bath towels embroidered in *Mon Chat* (mannishly beige) or *Ma Chatte* (a ladylike mauve); and Limoges feeding dishes. I spent more than a moment over a miniature throne of gilded wood, with an armorial motif emblazoned on its velvet cushion with tinsel, sequins, and that scintillating powdery gook that ballet dancers use on their hair in *Swan Lake*.

La vendeuse thought she had a sucker and gushed. "I know, madame, that you have a *Roi Chat* at home, and *that* should be for him!"

"It would not suit the décor of my dining room," I said. "May we see the sweaters?"

That forced her to show me the *rayon des tricots*. Madame viewed her stock, piled neatly but extravagantly in the *vitrine*. "Is it for *le sport*? Or perhaps *la maison*? *Le voyage*? For *le soir* we have a divine little Italian thing, hand-crocheted with paillettes."

She brought out a ghastly golden garment that nearly blinded me. It looked like something you would see at a night club in Miami, except that its sleeves were ever so short, its back ever so long, and the part that was to accommodate the chest had two minuscule falsies attached "for an effect."

"Just imagine this on a *bête noire*," she ventured.

"Just a minute, madame," I managed to say. "Is there anything for a gentleman cat? Simple, unadorned, truly *pour le sport*?"

"Aha!" she cried. "A gentleman cat! I have *le mot juste*!"

Then she produced a cable-stitch turtleneck as red as a stop sign. "*Le dernier cri!* The demand is tremendous. It's what *they* are all wearing."

I was overcome with nausea, but managed a strangled, "And *who* are *they*?"

"*They*, madame, are *they*, the world of fashion, the dictators of taste, the pace setters!"

That woman was just plain sick in the head, or her customers were, dressing animals in those idiotic costumes.

Not that dressing animals up hasn't been going on for a long time. Grandville,[2] in the nineteenth century, togged them out in satins and brocades, gloved their paws, plumed their hats, and put them in a variety of situations that mocked the mores of his time.

And certainly I don't have to mention *Puss in Boots*—or the other

[2] Jean Ignace Isidore Gérard, French caricaturist, generally known by the pseudonym of Grandville. His success was made with *Métamorphoses du jour* (1828), a series of seventy scenes in which individuals with the bodies of men and faces of animals play the human comedy.

graphic transvestitism of artists who have dressed up animals in buttons and bows, and lavender and old lace, to caricature the human race.

Or the vaudevillians or circus people. It was a sure laugh on the Keith time to put a tutu around the middle of a fox terrier—or a sunbonnet and a bustle on a Mama Poodle. And they were not above putting baby poodles in swaddling clothes.

And in how many acts were there dogs who were dressed as firemen—or even as brides?

They never got a cat to stand still for any of this nonsense.

The passion to dress animals has lately taken on an entirely new aspect. I was looking at Paul Coates's program on television one night last spring. He is an interviewer who asks questions in depth of all sorts of odd people. The oddest man he ever had on his program was one who represented SENA—Society to End Nakedness in Animals.

I listened and laughed and thought it merely a kooky stunt. And then I listened more carefully, and now I'm not quite sure.

The representative for SENA seemed very serious indeed, almost a philosopher, as he campaigned for SENA's goal "to put clothes on all members of the animal world who have the misfortune to circulate in human society." For the record, SENA's motto is: "Decency today means morality tomorrow."

I know you'll be glad to hear that SENA's primary concerns are dogs, cats, horses, and cows, since these are the animals most American children see on a day-to-day basis. Birds, which are naturally modest, are not in SENA's ken. The organization claims to have between thirty and forty thousand followers in the United States, and is principally financed by a substantial legacy from a gentleman who was deeply devoted to the cause. In the end, these evangelists plan to ask Congress to pass a law requiring suitable garments for all animals.

As you are beginning to see, it's a tossup whether the anti-animal people are crazier than the pro-animal people. Not much of a tossup, actually, because the anti-animal people are in so small a minority —and most of them keep their mouths shut. The pro-animal people, on the other hand, sometimes go beyond the bounds of sanity.

When, in my morning mail, last winter, I received this invitation, I knew I was close to the nadir.

Dr. and Mrs. C—— L——

request the honor of your presence at

A Catnip Cocktail Party

On Saturday, the fourteenth of February, at

1127 L—— V—— Drive

Pasadena, California

In honor of

GRIGRI

On the occasion of her sixteenth birthday

and to wish her Bon Voyage on her first trip to Mexico

R.S.V.P.

When, in the same mail, I found the same invitation addressed to Mr. Louis XIV Roth, I knew I was finally plumbing the depths.

Grigri is a cat, of course.

I agreed to go, only to see what new excesses were to be reached. But I decided firmly against taking Louis, and so told my hostess over the telephone.

"The party," she said icily, "is not for people. It's for cats."

"But Louis isn't feeling very well," I said lamely. "Mayn't I come without him?"

"If Louis isn't feeling well," she said, "you may certainly *not* come. The last thing we need at Grigri's birthday party is Typhoid Mary."

"It's nothing serious," I insisted. "More mental than anything else."

"In that case," said my hostess, "what he really needs is contact with other cats."

"I don't believe in *that*," I said.

"I've felt for a long time that you've been frustrating Louis," she replied firmly and with an authoritative tone in her voice. "After all, cats aren't people; they need other cats to play with. And I was looking forward to having him tell Grigri what it's like to travel. However, if you insist on segregating him . . ."

What had started out as a lame excuse turned into a lecture on the mental health of the lonely cat. When she got to the point where she was discussing *my* gregariousness or lack of it as a way of life, I cut in to admit I was cornered. Utterly defeated, I agreed to make a personal appearance with Louis.

The idea is to make such an appearance with all the other "nannies," leave your present, twick the birthday girl under the chin, and leave before sex rears its ugly head and the fighting starts.

I must explain my use of the word "nanny." A few years ago a fascinating book was published in England, *The Barford Cat Affair*. Strangely enough, it has nothing to do with cats—that is, cats as we know them, as cats. In the book the cats, as cats, are the people and the people, as people, are the cats, if you know what I mean, and I'm not sure *I* do. In any case, throughout the story the cats and people switch roles, and as a result the cats refer to the people they live with as "housekeepers." I don't really feel I'm Louis's housekeeper; a more accurate term would be governess or nanny.

As a good nanny, I had to get Grigri a little something because no combination birthday and bon voyage party, whether for cat or human, is complete without a present. It's a difficult task to find something for the Man Who Has Everything, but every once in a while a high-style jeweler will come through with a solid gold toothpick or sterling silver typewriter keys, or somebody will offer a room-sized vicuña rug. The Cat Who Has Everything is another matter. The cat who has *four* of everything is a crisis.

A visit to a series of pet shops left me uninspired. Cat toys, like nutcrackers, haven't changed in years. The catnip mice in their gray flannel coats, the hideous yarn pompons with the little bell inside, the ghastly pink celluloid balls that roll under furniture, never to be seen again, are all quite out of the question. For a moment I wished to be back in Paris in my incredible cat boutique. I'd *buy* that blue feather boa! But I wasn't going to fall into any cat-fool trap. I compromised by sending a contribution in Grigri's name to the Children's Fund of UNESCO, which is the perfect gift for Anyone Who Has Everything.

So Louis and I arrived that Saturday afternoon at a house in Pasadena, not in the least surprised to see the Cadillacs and Continentals lined up. We gave our Buick into the hands of an eager parking boy.

"You got a cat, lady?" he asked.

"I got a cat, son," I said.

"Good," he said, "because nobody allowed in without a cat."

I smiled and carried Louis in, but I heard him say to a colleague, "Another one of them nuts!"

And the colleague replied, "I feel like I'm in a loony bin, like."

Grigri's party began with a reception line for all of us nuts from the loony bin. We queued up with our charges under our arms to greet "the little old lady." I was at the end of the line, having arrived late, and could not see what was happening up front. Unfortunately, I was not warned about the scene I was about to witness. There was Grigri in her cage, dressed as Whistler's mother, in tippet bonnet, fichu, cameo, and gray bengaline, sitting on a doll's rocking chair. To make matters worse, her "nanny" had framed the little cage in a baroque molding. The effect was so startling that I fled the receiving line for the people's bar—feeling the same horror Red Riding Hood must have felt when she saw the wolf in her grandmother's bed.

Our hostess suggested that each of us hold onto his cat with a lead during the festivities. In that way the grand march to the cats' refreshment table would be less confusing. All the cats got the scent of the freshly poached cod at the same time and headed for it. I kicked off my shoes and, clinging to Louis's leash, dashed with them. All the seating arrangements were upset as the cats jumped on the table. The cod disappeared at once, every bowl licked clean.

Now the pièce de résistance arrived—the birthday cake! Four layers of chopped liver with a garniture of sour cream. The honoree, still in her Whistler getup, more ghastly than ever, now that she stood on all four paws, was allowed to have the first lick. We held our cats back as the venerable old lady performed this rite. It was a touching moment, but only a moment. Then all hell broke loose.

I gathered Louis and ran, leaving a tangle of ladies, and leashes, and cats, and chopped liver, that I've no power to describe. I hear that the Fire Department had to be called to quell the riot with one of their hoses.

When Louis is sixteen, what I certainly will *not* do is to have a cocktail party for him like all the other cat fools.

Just a simple reception will have to do.

CHAPTER TWENTY-ONE

The
Cat
Hotel

It took me months to get over the Pasadena party. I kept wondering if that was how *I* looked to other people, and I decided it was. I also decided to reform.

I'm afraid it wasn't a very firm decision because when my husband came home one night and said that we must now go to England my first reaction was: "What about the English quarantine laws? What about Louis? How can we get him into England?"

"We can't," he said, which I considered a very dumb answer. "I'm afraid we'll just have to leave him behind."

I looked miserable, and then he said the terrible sentence that I'd heard so often, but never from him. "We've both got to realize he's only a cat."

Only a cat! Those three words seemed to sum up the whole problem. Like my Pasadena friend, was it true that I'd been reading something into Louis that wasn't there—that I'd been using him as a replacement for a child? Was it true that he was *only* a cat? I underwent a long period of soul searching—and then, with reality too much, I took refuge in fantasy. Perhaps the British had changed their laws. Perhaps the House of Commons had amended the old statutes. Perhaps Her Majesty, as passionate a horse lover as I, had intervened in the parliamentary process. I had a dream that if I called the consul he'd say, "I'm glad you called, madam. The quarantine law has been altered for the better. Her Majesty's Government will be more lenient in the future."

That wasn't what he said. In his sharp, precise voice he assured me that the quarantine law was still in effect and would continue to be in the foreseeable future.

That left me only two possibilities. I either left Louis behind, or I would have to find a way to smuggle him into England. I suspected that, as a smuggler, I wouldn't be much good, though I must say I considered a number of cloak-and-dagger possibilities and discarded them.

There was a third alternative, but one I instantly rejected; I could let my husband go and I could stay behind with Louis. But that meant that I was choosing between them.

"Did anybody ever have a more appalling problem?" I asked my manicurist.

She looked at me peculiarly. "I don't understand you," she said. "After all, it's only a cat."

Well, there I was. I sat down and had a long talk with myself and decided that I would leave Louis behind. However reluctantly, however painfully, I would leave him behind. And when I make up my mind, it's subject to change without notice. But where to leave him?

Then I remembered the advice given me at the time the French wouldn't allow cats into their country. Lillian Berk had recommended a place called Blackford's Hotel for Cats. I found her telephone number and called her, and the rave she put on about Blackford's made me imagine that this could be his ad:[1]

Resort hotel in the heart of Westwood, the home of the University of California. Six miles from the Pacific Ocean, easy access to the San Diego Freeway. Pleasant surroundings. Home cooking. Radio. Television. Spacious rooms, all with bath. Sunny patios. Restricted clientele. Reservations necessary. Diners' Club cards honored.

BLACKFORD'S HOTEL FOR CATS
2327 Cotner Avenue
Los Angeles, California

To hear Mrs. Berk tell it, Blackford's Hotel was Claridge's with cat desk clerks and bellboys. I had a vision of a vast lobby with cat hotel "dicks" and clients checking in and out with mounds of cat-size Louis Vuitton luggage. Persian lady cats would stroll

1 Of course, he doesn't advertise at all.

through the potted palms and well-dressed gentlemen Siamese would be sitting in the cocktail lounge, their tails draped around the bar stools, renewing old friendships over saucers of cream.

Then, as it must to all hotels, the time would come when its name would be changed to the Blackford-Hilton.

So I called up Blackford's and made some hesitant inquiries. Mr. Blackford, who has had a vast experience with cat keepers and their "kids"[2] must have recognized the indecision in my voice.

"Honey, why don't you come out and see the place first, alone?" he suggested amiably. "You can tell me all your troubles and I can tell you mine."

What I saw as I pulled up to the curb in front of 2327 Cotner Avenue was a simple, neatly painted little stucco building with a *No Vacancy* sign in its window. There was nothing "big city" about it. If anything, it looked more like a middle-class boardinghouse in a small Kansas town.

I rang a bell at a side gate, according to the directions on a little sign. A buzzer opened the door, which locked securely in back of me. It reminded me of the days when I was a Red Cross nurse's aide, working in the psychopathic ward at a Veterans' Administration hospital, and I shuddered. Those doors used to click and lock behind me in the same way.

I found myself in a charming little alley, beautifully planted with healthy tropical plants. A fountain trickled to my right and porcelain and ceramic cats played hide-and-seek among the rubber plants and Hawaiian ferns. Another door and another buzzer. Now I came back to face with the Ninth Wonder of the World.

This, indeed, was a cat hotel.

In front of me were two enclosed patios, filled with cats of every description. Some slept on cushions, others on the branches of a tree. A few were at the community drinking fountain, a few more conversing in a corner quietly, peacefully, hardly disturbed when an intruder entered their Nirvana.

Blackie came toward me with a grin on his face.[3] He unlocked the screen door that separated the cats' quarters from the outside.

"Well, how do you like it?" A calico cat was underfoot. "Hey, Cookie," said he, "go back to sleep. You were up late last night."

---

[2] "Kids" is Blackie's name for cats—don't blame it on *me.*
[3] I have a right to call him Blackie *now* because I'm *in.* I passed his rigid test of cat love and my dossier is clean.

Then to me, "That's Meredith Willson's cat, Cookie. She always comes here when he does a show in New York."

Cookie looked radiantly happy. "Doesn't she miss the Willsons?" I was rapidly coming to the point of my visit. One forlorn cat and away I'd go. That was to be my measuring stick. Just one forlorn cat.

"Miss the Willsons?" Blackie laughed. "When they come to get her, she won't go."

I'm afraid I considered *that* pure salesmanship.

"May I look around?" I asked formally.

"Sure as shootin'," said Blackie, not so formally. "But there's no use really discussing this matter until I find out about you and your cat. At the moment, I don't even have a vacancy. Now I'm expecting one in the next couple of days, and I've got a lot of reservations."

"But my case is an emergency," I said.

"Well," said Blackie, "I'm always prepared to take care of emergencies—if they're really and truly emergencies. Now, exactly what's your problem?"

"Well," I said falteringly, "I have a cat who is accustomed to— I don't quite know how to put it—but he's spoiled. He's a terror. He's never been with other cats. I've always taken him with me whenever I traveled—but this time I can't."

"England," said Blackie flatly.

"England," said I, just as flatly.

"Can't understand England," said Blackie.

"Well, it's a question of rabies," I said. "There once was a problem in France, you know, but I did everything I could. I plagued the French government until I——"

"Oh, you're *that* Mrs. Roth," Blackie said, his eyes lighting up. "Well, in that case, any cat of yours would be a welcome guest here."

"You know me?" I asked, flushing gently.

"Lady," he said, "everybody who brings a cat in here knows you. Some folks even say you practically caused a revolution in France."

I demurred. "I simply called a few matters to their attention," I said shyly.

"You ought to do the same thing in England," he said. "Now let me show you what it is to really live—that is, if you're a cat."

So he took me on a tour of the premises. And it was scored

musically. The sound of violins came through an amplifier. The tunes of Rodgers and Hart and Chopin filled the corridors.

"Here is where they live." Blackie showed me the cubicles that lined the wall. Each was about six feet square, and furnished with a bath mat, a shelf, and a large plastic sand tray. Most of the cats were taking a siesta in the patio, but the few who remained in their cages were relaxed and content. Blackie called each one by name and had something to say about the individual's personal problems.

"Hy, Mr. Blue, you got a letter from Paris today?" He showed me a letter with a Paris postmark that was attached to the wire of Mr. Blue's cage. "He's Fritz Lang's cat but he has such a good time here that they treat him to a vacation every year."

A large black and white alley cat came forward to have his ears scratched. "That's Arthur. He belongs to an air force colonel stationed in England, and *you* know what that means. Next month the colonel goes to Italy, and I'll send Arthur over."

We visited the kitchen, a dream in stainless steel. "Here's where I do my cooking and cutting." He opened a cupboard door. In it were cans of the finest salmon, shrimp, lobster, and clams. "Just in case," said Blackie, "one of the kids gets a hankerin'."

He opened a refrigerator filled with liver, kidney, heart, and melt of horse, beef, and lamb. "I got to keep it all. You never know what someone will want."

Blackie talked a lot but it was good talk for a worrier, and all, of course, calculated to reduce the tension. He pointed to a chubby little taupe-colored kitten.

"Three months old? Isn't he a little large for his age?" I asked.

"Hell, no! He's a bobcat. I picked him up in the Hollywood hills after a fire. You can bet your bottom dollar his ma wasn't around. I'm going to raise him like one of the kids. Now when I was in Burma . . ."

Blackie was a good psychologist. Instead of discussing his hotel, he talked about Burma and Tanganyika and the big cats and the little ones. We went from cheetahs to ocelots, from Abyssinians to Siamese. I had almost forgotten why I came, until Blackie suddenly asked me what Louis ate. As I talked, he took notes. "Cut the kidney, not too fine," I said. "Heart once a week; liver once a week. Scald it first. White meat tuna. Chunky. Poached haddock or cod, filleted, of course."

"Your kid seems to have a nice palate. So, if you want him to come here, we want to have him."

"You're sure?"

"Positive."

"Anything else I ought to know?"

"Nothing except we love cats, and we've got some house rules."

"House rules?"

Blackie thereupon announced the house rules in a stern voice:

1. No worrying about your kid.
2. A letter a week come hell or high water.
3. Enteritis shots for the kid.
4. Pneumonitis shots for the kid.
5. No sex allowed. (Altered cats *only*.)

Blackie's point No. 5, which gave him a peculiarly restricted clientele, was (and is) a safety measure to insure some degree of decorum when cats of two sexes share a party wall. He did not deny that fighting went on, sex or no sex. "Gee, every once in a while the kids scrap over something." As he spoke, a cacophony sounded from the patio.

"Shut up out there. What's going on?"

I followed him to the source of the trouble. A Siamese and an Abyssinian were pulling a pillow apart. The kapok was flying and it seemed as though a few of the cats were coming to tell Blackie what the fight was about. Blackie didn't have to be told. He picked up each of the quarreling cats, whispered something into their ears, put them down again, and that was that. It was peaceful again, even though the kapok blizzard still raged.

Blackie's back was turned to me and for the first time (although it was there all the time) I noticed the emblem emblazoned across the back of his windbreaker: an ocelot (rampant) with the motto: "Ocelot Club of America."

I asked about it.

"A lot of people keep them. Ocelots," said Blackie. "You'd be surprised at the membership of our club."

Then I remembered the washing machine repairman who came to our house one day to do something about the suds. Louis sniffed him suspiciously. "Have you got a cat?" I asked.

"Gosh, *no*, but there's a lady over on Wetherly who's got the same trouble as you, and she's got the biggest darn cat I ever saw, with spots all over."

I repeated this conversation verbatim to Blackie. He wasn't a bit surprised.

"Oh, that one. I know him. That's Rowdy. A hell of a cat that is, too. I gotta call that lady up. She missed two meetings of our Ocelot Club and we can't have that kind of thing."

I was having a good time. I liked Blackie. I liked the hotel. I liked the cats, but would Louis? "Stop rationalizing," I said to myself. "He's only a cat. He'll probably love it."

Two days later I gave Blackie the custody of Louis. I saw him put into the large cage. I saw his leash hung on the outside. I saw his name on a card above the door. Of course there were tears in my eyes. Of course I had *mille regrets*.

"Don't forget to write," insisted Blackie. "Once a week at least. You know, they can tell the letter is from *you*. I put it in the cage and, by golly, they sniff and sniff. They sure get the message." Blackie put his arm around me. "Honey, I know you're going to worry. Don't. He'll be okay and tonight he'll get his cooked cod."

"Do you think he'll forget me?"

Blackie has great confidence in cats. "Forget you? I'll take even money that you forget him first."

"How dare you?"

"I was kidding," he said. "Listen, if you can't live without him, just cable and I'll send him to you."

This time the door clicked behind me and I was on the street. Cat hairs still clung to my traveling suit. My plane for London was to leave late that evening from the International Airport in Los Angeles. There was still time to see Louis once more on my way to the airport for, by some divine providence, Blackford's Hotel for Cats was on a street that ran parallel to Sepulveda Boulevard, the direct route. I forced myself *not* to stop. I phoned, instead, from the airport, as Blackie knew full well I would.

"The kids are all asleep, even Louis. I know it'll make you unhappy, but he doesn't miss you a bit. Ate his dinner. Used his box and talked to the guy next door—you remember Arthur, the colonel's cat . . ."

The hell with the colonel's cat! He didn't miss me a bit!

CHAPTER TWENTY-TWO

London

Nor did I miss him.

Well, perhaps that's going a *bit* far. I was very busy helping my husband—trips to the laboratory twice a day with film contact prints and instructions—and trying to turn our tiny little flat in Red Lion Yard into a home in the English spring.

Not an easy thing to do, living in England, fighting with the daily woman to lay the fires (at a time of the calendar when fires are not *supposed* to be laid, madam), trying to deal with a hot-water heater that was used originally by Watt in his experiments on the steam engine, and marketing. Oh, marketing is all very well in London if you give your custom to Harrod's or Fortnum's; marketing is strenuous work when you patronize the neighborhood shops and have to carry everything home. Oh, how I longed for one of those carts from Safeway.

So you see I was pretty busy—without Louis—and I tried very hard not to think of him.

But why did there have to be so many cats in London to remind me of him? Just when I thought I had him out of my mind, the ginger cat in the fruiterer's in Shepherd's Market would rub her ears against me as I waited for my purchase, and I would dissolve.

Then there was the unfortunate timing of the Cat Show at Olympia. I decided not to go, went, and walked through the aisles of cages shedding a tear for every Siamese I saw.

Then I realized that I'd been kidding myself. My loneliness for Louis was deep and awful. Let me put it another way. My *loneliness* was deep and awful. My acquaintance in London was select but small; my husband was at the studio most of the day; I loathed housekeeping. I do it well, mind you, but I absolutely loathe it. It's only bearable if I have somebody to talk to. British TV is not my cup of tea; British radio is very somber. I had to have some living thing I could talk to while I tried to peel those potatoes.

So I considered buying a kitten, a little Siamese, which I would eventually take home to Louis.

I saw an ad in the agony column of the London *Times* and called the lady up. I was as polite as polite could be; I even broadened my *a* a little, but the lady at the other end of the phone was not fooled for an instant. She was huffy.

"I'd never sell one of my kittens to an American," she said. "You people know *nothing* about taking care of cats. Just feed them out of tins. Your veterinaries are charlatans. And you know, dear, you never even inoculate."

"Not true. Not true," I spluttered. "That's the grossest anti-American propaganda."

"I'm not political," said the lady shrilly. "I simply love cats."

"So do I," I shouted. But it was too late. She'd hung up.

I was not happy with the British.

One Sunday morning, at Marble Arch, my attitude softened. There was a speaker protesting from a soapbox about the sudden influx of foreign animals that was undermining the health of English livestock. Apparently the quarantine did not apply to anything but pets. In any case, England was faced with an epidemic of hoof and mouth disease, courtesy of some Argentine bulls brought over to breed with Lancashire cows.

"Let's keep foreign animals out of England," proclaimed the speaker, "otherwise all our English cattle will die."

"Bully for you," shouted the man next to me, and then looked at me inquiringly.

Because I am Mrs. Caspar Milquetoast, I found myself shouting, "Bully for you."

Then I saw an item in the *Express* that settled it—cats were definitely things of the past.

JET ENGINE NOISE PROVES
A RODENT EXTERMINATOR

Hordes of field mice around Waggum airfield long had plagued neighboring farmers and field officials. But soon after four French-built Alouette jet helicopters were stationed at the small field recently, the small rodents died by the droves.

Scientists gave the puzzled but pleased residents the answer: The jets' engine noise is of an unusually high frequency fatal to the rodents.

What a world we *do* live in! How I long for 1916!

That was the tenor of the letter I sat down to write to Louis. It seemed an item that might interest him. But, even as I thought so, I felt an utter, utter fool. Perhaps others of Blackford's clients could write letters to their cats; I couldn't. I could write a letter to Blackford and tell *him*, but as for writing to Louis directly—well, even my maladjustment isn't that maladjusted.

I remembered that I was not the only one. Meredith Willson once told me about a crisis with his wife, Rini. They, too, had left their cat, Cookie, at Blackford's for the first time and had received his strict instructions to write weekly. Meredith noticed Rini sitting at her desk in their New York hotel room, depressed and dejected, staring at nothing at all.

"What's wrong, darling?" asked Meredith. "Are you ill?"

Rini came out of her trance. "Ill? Wrong? I'm just wondering what to write to our cat."

Rini settled for a postcard. I did the same thing.

And there I was, with a pen in my hand and all that lovely blue note paper, and I took to a little hobby I'd often used instead of crossword puzzles—writing rhymes. The first one, of course, was about a cat.

LONDON SANS LOUIS

Pussycat, pussycat, where have you been?
I've not been to London to visit the Queen!
But I've been to Paris and Capri and Rome.
I've had my saucer of cream at the Dôme!
I've never been asked to afternoon tea,
Her Majesty frowns upon creatures like me.

And that led me logically to writing about other animals—mostly in the London Zoo.

THE TORTOISE

The giant tortoise weighs a ton
And never really has much fun,
Hampered by his massive shell,
He makes love rarely, and not well.

THE MONGOOSE

The mongoose is a fearless battler
Of python, boa, krait and rattler.
After fighting, he, the winner
Has his woeful snake for dinner.

THE ALLIGATOR

"It's better to be wet than dead,"
Says the alligator from his bed.
"To fight is right, but I may lose
And end up as a pair of shoes."

I had a dream that somebody would publish them, but in my heart I knew nobody would. Still, it was a way to spend some time.

It was a challenge to find rhymes for tapir and wallaby, but, just as I succeeded, a new animal would come into my life. Friends in London, who were all amateur zoologists, would say, "What did you do about Bosman's potto?"

Well, here's what I did about the potto:

BOSMAN'S POTTO[1]

The potto was the envy of
Chopin and Rachmaninoff.
Unfortunately, he can't be taught
To play on a pianoforte.

These little mammals with their prehensile tails were completely unknown to me. Either the Prospect Park and Central Park zoos were derelict in their duties, or I had never noticed them before. One day as I was standing in front of a Bosman's potto, a nice young man spoke to me.

"Charming, aren't they?"

I agreed that they were ever so charming and added, "So unusual."

"Unusual?" He was astounded that I had used the word. "My dear," he continued, "I have *two* at home."

[1] The potto (*Perodicticus potto*) is part of the sloth family. He resembles a kinkajou but has the most amazing little hands in the world with a 180-degree angle between his index finger and thumb. Long enough to reach two octaves on a keyboard.

"You mean they can be pets?"

"Under the proper conditions, yes."

"What are the proper conditions?"

"First you must observe them. What do you see? Quite. They're in a tree. That's all they ask. Well, that and a vegetarian diet. Fruits and vegetables and a marshmallow once in a while."

I didn't like to ask, but I did. "Can they be housebroken?"

The nice young man blushed. "Eventually," he whispered. "Eventually."

The pottos seemed like dear little things, cuddly and soft, with curious human hands no larger than a ten-cent piece. Their long arms were curled around the branch of the little tree in their cage. Then, I seriously thought of getting one for myself as a pet.

"Do you think I could find one?" I asked the nice young man. "Without going to Madagascar?"

"Quite! Without going to Madagascar!"

He knew where one was presumably obtainable. Somewhere in Hammersmith. Difficult to find. Would I meet him in front of St. Martin's in the Fields on Saturday morning tennish? I said I would, and as I left the small mammal house, I wondered how I could break the news to my husband that Louis was to be replaced, just temporarily, of course, with a Bosman's potto. I rehearsed all the answers. They would be the same questions I had heard since I was four when I brought my first stray kittens home.

1. "Are you prepared to accept the responsibility?"
"Yes."
2. "Do you promise to feed it and care for it?"
"Yes."
3. "What happens when we leave for the country?" (In this case, it would be: "What happens when we leave for home?")

For that, I had prepared a very mature answer. "I shall present him to the Los Angeles Zoo."

I overflowed with civic pride at the idea of giving my city such a rare animal. I could almost see the little brass plate over the cage: "Bosman's Potto. Habitat, Madagascar. Gift of Mrs. Sanford Roth."

I left my news for after dinner. To soften the blow, I grilled some very expensive Scottish lamb, served an outrageously good St. Emilion, and topped dinner with a strawberry tart from Fortnum's.

As for the savory, well, you know what you can do with those sardines.

As my husband lit his Gauloise cigarette, I said, "Darling, I have some news for you, I——"

I didn't have the opportunity to finish the sentence because he was saying at the same time, "Darling, I have some news for you——

"Yours first, darling."

"No, *yours* first, darling."

I started with, "Darling, I have an appointment Saturday morning at ten——"

He interrupted. "Saturday morning at ten? You won't be able to keep it, darling; we're going to Paris for three months."

Paris! Three months! *Darling!*

CHAPTER TWENTY-THREE

Reunion

Mr. Blackie Blackford
Blackford's Hotel for Cats
2327 Cotner Avenue
Los Angeles, California
PLEASE SEND LOUIS POSTHASTE. AIR MAIL. SPECIAL DELIVERY. IN
GREATEST POSSIBLE LUXURY AND COMFORT TO ORLY AIRPORT, PARIS.
NOTIFY ME WHAT PLANE. LOVE TO LOUIS. REGARDS TO YOU.

Beulah Roth

Mrs. Sanford Roth
Red Lion Yard
London, England
IMPOSSIBLE GET RESERVATIONS UNTIL WEEK FROM WEDNESDAY ON PAN
AM.

Blackie Blackford

Mr. Blackie Blackford
Blackford's Hotel for Cats
2327 Cotner Avenue
Los Angeles, California
TRY SAS.

Beulah Roth

Mrs. Sanford Roth
Red Lion Yard
London, England
SAS CROWDED.

Blackie Blackford

Mr. Blackie Blackford
Blackford's Hotel for Cats
2327 Cotner Avenue
Los Angeles, California
TRY TWA.

Beulah Roth

Mrs. Sanford Roth
Red Lion Yard
London, England
TWA BOOKED SOLID. IT IS THE HEIGHT OF THE TOURIST SEASON.

Blackie Blackford

Mr. Dore Schary
33 East 70th Street
New York, N.Y.
DEAR DORE: DO YOU KNOW HOWARD HUGHES? LOVE.

Beulah

Mrs. Sanford Roth
Red Lion Yard
London, England.
WHY?

Dore

Mr. Dore Schary
33 East 70th Street
New York, N.Y.
IF YOU HAVE ANY INFLUENCE WITH HIM, COULD YOU MANAGE TO GET
SPACE FOR MY CAT AS SOON AS POSSIBLE ABOARD ONE OF HIS TWA
AIRCRAFTS TO PARIS?

Beulah

Mrs. Sanford Roth
Red Lion Yard
London, England
LOTS OF SPACE FOR PEOPLE BUT NONE FOR CATS. HAVE WIRED HUGHES.
LOVE.

Dore

Mr. Dore Schary
33 East 70th Street
New York, N.Y.
THANKS. YOU'RE A DOLL. LOVE TO MIRIAM.

Beulah

Mrs. Sanford Roth
Red Lion Yard
London, England.
MR. SCHARY'S ADVICE TO MR. HUGHES RECEIVED. SPECIAL ARRANGE-
MENTS WILL BE MADE.

TWA

Mrs. Sanford Roth
Red Lion Yard
London, England
LOUIS WILL LEAVE TWA FLIGHT NUMBER SEVEN CONNECTING IN NEW
YORK WITH FLIGHT NUMBER NINE. ARRIVE PARIS THREE PM, TUESDAY,
MAY TWENTY-SECOND.

Blackie Blackford

Mr. Blackie Blackford
Blackford's Hotel for Cats
2327 Cotner Avenue
Los Angeles, California
HOW LONG IS STOPOVER IN NEW YORK?

Beulah Roth

Mrs. Sanford Roth
Red Lion Yard
London, England.
FIVE HOURS.

Blackie Blackford

Miss Sadie Ratner
576 Eastern Parkway
Brooklyn, N.Y.
DEAR AUNT SADIE, COULD YOU ARRANGE MEET LOUIS, KEEP HIM COM-
PANY, INTERNATIONAL AIRPORT, DURING STOPOVER? BE SURE AND LET
ME KNOW IF IT'S TOO MUCH TROUBLE.

Beulah

Mrs. Sanford Roth
Red Lion Yard
London, England
ARE YOU OUT OF YOUR MIND? I LOVE LOUIS AND WELCOME CHANCE TO
CHAT WITH HIM.

                                        Aunt Sadie

Miss Sadie Ratner
576 Eastern Parkway
Brooklyn, N.Y.
YOU'RE A DARLING. BRING SOME LAMB MEAT AND TWO DEVEINED
SHRIMP OR AS ALTERNATE FOUR OUNCES CALF'S LIVER WHITE AROUND
EDGES.

                                        Beulah

Mrs. Sanford Roth
Red Lion Yard
London, England
LOUIS ARRIVED NEW YORK IN BEST OF HEALTH. ATE SHRIMP. PLANE
DELAYED SEVEN HOURS BECAUSE OF ELECTRIC STORM. HAVE TAKEN HIM
HOME WITH ME.

                                        Aunt Sadie

Miss Sadie Ratner
576 Eastern Parkway
Brooklyn, N.Y.
YOU'RE A DARLING.

                                        Beulah

Mrs. Sanford Roth
Red Lion Yard
London, England.
PLANE WILL ARRIVE NINE PM PARIS.

                                        Aunt Sadie

She was wrong about 9:00 P.M. It was eleven-ten, and twenty
minutes more before all the luggage was deposited and then, suddenly, he was in my arms. And there never has been such a reunion
since the famous one in Vienna.

"All of this time you've been waiting for a cat?" asked the lady standing next to me.

"Yes," I said. "A cat."

"Well, my dear," said the lady, "I don't know whether you've ever traveled with a cat . . ." and she went on before I could stop her, "but you're going to have a good deal of trouble finding sand in Paris. . . . As for sawdust, it's very hard to get. I suggest the pet shops along the Quai Mégisserie, which sell everything from chipmunks to cheetahs, and there it's possible to obtain a lovely white coral sand . . ."

"Madame," I said, "you must be a blood sister. How old is your cat?"

"Cat?" She looked puzzled, and then she smiled. "Well," she said, "Aphrodite is fourteen, Medea is thirteen, Minerva is twelve, Juno's eleven. . . ."

She had thirty-six in all. So you see I *am* an amateur.

How to
Say It
in French and Italian

If you travel in either Italy or France, there are a lot of words you're going to have to know. Here, at least, are some of them.

IN GENERAL

	FRENCH	ITALIAN
Male cat	Chat	Gatto
Female cat	Chatte	Gatta
Alley cat	Chat gouttière	Gatto smarrito
His wife	Chatte gouttière	Gatta smarrita
Little cat (male)	Petit chat	Gattino
Little cat (female)	Petite chatte	Gattina
Spoiled cat (yours)	Chat gâté	Gatto sciupato
Altered cat	Chat coupé	Gatto castrato
(Avoid the subject)		
Cat Apache	Matou	"Dolce vita"
Will he bite me?	Est-ce qu'il est	E cattivo?
Is he bad?	méchant?	
Sawdust		
	Sciure	Segatura
	(pronounced seeyawr)	

AT THE MARKET

	FRENCH	ITALIAN
Butcher shop selling what cats eat and gourmets love	*Triperie*	*Tripperia*
Butcher shop	*Boucherie*	*Macelleria*
The butcher	*Boucher*	*Macellaio*
Horsemeat butcher shop	*Boucherie chevaline*	*Macelleria cavallo*
Beef	*Boeuf*	*Manzo*
Beefsteak	*Bifteck*	*Bistecca*
Heart	*Coeur*	*Cuore*
Beef heart	*Coeur de boeuf*	*Cuore di manzo*
Veal heart	*Coeur de veau*	*Cuore di vitello*
Lamb heart	*Coeur de mouton*	*Cuore di agnello*
Calf's liver	*Foie de veau*	*Fegato di vitello*
Beef liver	*Foie de boeuf*	*Fegato di manzo*
Lamb liver	*Foie de mouton*	*Fegato di pecora*
Beef melt (spleen)	*Rate de boeuf*	*Milza di manzo*
Veal melt	*Rate de veau*	*Milza di vitello*
Lamb melt	*Rate de mouton*	*Milza di agnello*[1]
Beef kidneys	*Rognons de boeuf*[2]	*Rognoni di manzo*
Veal kidneys	*Rognons de veau*[2]	*Rognoni di vitello*
Lamb kidneys	*Rognons de mouton*[2]	*Rognoni di agnello*[3]
Fish	*Poisson*	*Pesce*[4]
Salmon	*Saumon*	*Salmone*
Trout	*Truite*	*Trota*
Sole	*Sole*	*Sogliola*
Pasteurized milk	*Lait pasteurisé*	*Latte fresco*[5]
Canned milk	*Lait en boite*	*Latte in scatola*
Cat crackers	*Biscuits des chats* (Obtainable in France. Brand names, "Félix" and "Minou.")	*Biscotti per i gatti* (Italy has them too!)
Grass	*Herbe*	*Erba*
A pot of grass	*Un pot de l'herbe* (Any florist sells this in Paris.)	*Vaso d'erba*
To eat grass	*Manger l'herbe*	*Mangiare l'erba*

[1] Lamb melt in Italy are too small to mention. They provide only an hors d'oeuvre for a cat.
[2] These are delicacies in France and may run into a pretty franc. They are sold in *boucheries*, not *triperies*.
[3] Lamb kidneys, like everything else that comes out of a lamb in Italy, are too small to be taken seriously.
[4] Do not confuse *pesca* (peach) with *pesce* (fish) or you'll have a hysterical fishmonger on your hands.
[5] Most milk is pasteurized in Italy.

AT THE VETERINARY

	FRENCH	ITALIAN
Sick	*Malade*	*Malato*
Fever	*Fièvre*	*Febbre*
Enteritis	*Entérite*	*Enterite*
Constipation	*Constipation*	*Costipazione*
Diarrhea	*Diarrhée*	*Diarrea*
Veterinary	*Vétérinaire*	*Veterinario*
A shot	*Piqûre*	*Puntura*
A pill	*Pilule*	*Pillola*
Health certificate	*Certificat de santé*	*Certificato di salute*
He has eaten a thread[6]	*Il a mangé du fil*	*A mangiato un filo*
He has swallowed a needle	*Il a mangé une aiguille*	*A mangiato un ago*
He has swallowed a bone	*Il a mangé un os*	*A mangiato un osso*
He has swallowed poison	*Il a mangé du poison*	*A mangiato del veleno*

[6] This is only a partial list of things a cat might eat, accidentally or purposely. Mice, rats, rabbits, grasshoppers, lizards, beetles, and crabs shouldn't make him sick enough to see a doctor.

IN A HOTEL

	FRENCH	ITALIAN
Superintendent or chief porter	*Concierge*	*Portiere*
Housemaid	*Femme de ménage* *Bonne*	*Donna di servizio* *Donna di casa*
Maid in a hotel	*Femme de chambre*	*Donna di camera*
Male chambermaid in a hotel	*Valet de chambre*	*Valletto di camera*
Do not disturb the cat	*Ne dérangez pas, s'il vous plaît, le chat*	*Non disturbate il gatto*
A room with a bath	*Une chambre avec salle de bain*	*Camera con bagno, per favore*
Room without a balcony	*Une chambre sans balcon*	*Camera senza balcone*
Room without a fireplace	*Une chambre sans cheminée*	*Camera senza camino*

IN A RESTAURANT

	FRENCH	ITALIAN
Something for the cat	*Quelque chose pour le chat*	*Qualcosa per il gatto*
Leftovers	*Restes de viande*	*Rimanenti di carne*
No gravy, please	*Sans sauce, s'il vous plaît*	*Senza salsa, per favore*
Hamburger	*Hamburger*	*Hamburger*
Raw meat	*Viande crue*	*Carne cruda*
Cooked meat	*Viande cuite*	*Carne cotta*
Medium	*Moyen*	*Mezzo e mezzo*
Rare	*Sanglant*	*Sanguinosa*

APPENDIX II

A
Cat Cookbook
for Travelers

These recipes have been culled from friends all over Europe and the United States. They are invaluable, both at home and abroad.

Some people say that a cat stops needing milk when his mother turns off the spigot. They say that about humans, too, but milk as a stomach soother, a quick pick-me-up, a thirst quencher, is unsurpassed. It does a great job, too, on a cat's intestinal tract when nervous tension makes him irregular.

For some silly reason cats prefer canned milk to the stuff that comes in bottles and not all cats like *that*. I've heard many cat "nannies" say that theirs won't touch it. If they won't, they won't, but you can always *try* by adding allure to it in the form of Pablum (sold internationally). All cats like to be treated as kittens once in a while, so try this before you resort to that laxative. An old lady in Cannes told me about this one:

BABY DAYS MILK (*Lait d'Enfance*)

½ cup undiluted evaporated milk
¼ cup warm water
About ¼ cup Pablum

Stir until it has the consistency of gruel. Offer it to your cat as an homage, a reward, or just because you like him. Leave him alone with it. Come back three minutes later: empty bowl, happy cat!

EGGS LOUIS XIV (*Oeufs Louis XIV*)

This is a favorite with my cat. I tried it once with leftover farina and he loved it. An easier way (without eating farina yourself) is to soak ½ cup of the filthy stuff in some boiling water until it forms a mush. You can use hot broth, milk, or tomato juice, too. To this add a beaten egg and a pinch of salt. Mix well and serve.

GOLDEN CHEESE (*Fromage Doré* or *Ricotta Dorata*)

This recipe was given to me by a Sicilian princess. She used ricotta but cottage cheese is just as good. A good cat portion is about ½ cup. Add the yolk of an egg and mix well. Remember to *chambrée* both egg and cottage cheese before serving.

YOGHURT

Yoghurt can be found wherever you are in supermarkets, dairies, *laiteries*, and *latterie*.

Chambréed, of course, it makes a wonderful substitute for milk. Some cats prefer it. Others think it is milk of magnesia. Put it into a saucer and hope for the best. It's supposed to make some marvelous improvements in the intestinal tract.

POULTRY

Please don't get up early in the morning to cook a chicken for a cat, *but* if you are doing a boiled bird for yourself, remember that cats will enjoy the skin more than the garbage man. Chicken skin, pinfeathers and all, minced into an otherwise unpalatable canned cat food will make all the difference in the world. It can turn a miserable pauper's repast into a feast.

Only in America are chicken gizzards or hearts to be found sold by the pound. Either we eat a lot of chicken or our chickens have two of everything. In Europe you must buy a chicken to get the gizzard. If you should run into some, boil them until tender, put them through your meat grinder, moisten with a little broth, and, *voilà*, perfection! Mix them with any canned food except fish. The idea may not bother cats but it seems unwise to me. A pound of gizzards makes a lot of cat food in case you have company.

All sorts of chicken parts are available in Europe, but the gizzards and hearts are the only ones recommended for cat use. The breasts are too expensive, the neck and wings too bony.

Chicken heads are *not quite* a food but they can give a cat a lot of fun. Maurice de Vlaminck first told me about this, but he lived on a farm and had a lot of cats and a lot of chickens. I can't guarantee what it will do to a town-house living room. If you want to see your cat giving an accurate imitation of a tiger attacking his prey, do this: get a chicken head somewhere (I admit they are rare in America these days), throw it to your cat, and *watch*. A well-known British veterinary insists that a cat needs feathers in his diet, but if *you* don't, then pluck some of the feathers off before serving. If I may make a suggestion, search the premises thoroughly when the cat shows signs of having enough of a good thing. The battered head (and it is *not* a pretty sight) may turn up behind a curtain or in your bed.

There is nothing in a chicken head to harm a cat, not even the bones. Actually, if you want to make a Frenchman happy, serve him a chicken brain. He will say, *"Formidable!"*

THE INNARDS

BEEF HEART (*Coeur de Boeuf*)

One heart is the same as another as far as nourishment is concerned, and the fact that some are smaller than others depends on the animal to whom it belonged. A beef heart can make a meal for three cats, a lamb heart offers just enough for one. Beef hearts seem to be available all the time, while calf and lamb hearts have their seasons.

One pound of beef heart will serve the average appetite three meals. It can be frozen, too, and brought out for a rainy day.

METHOD: Cut the heart into pieces that will fit into a meat grinder. Use the coarsest blade available. This doesn't squash the meat into nothingness, making it look like something it is *not*. If your cat prefers cooked food to raw, parboil the heart before it is chopped, until it becomes white around the edges. Ten minutes should accomplish this.

Raw heart may be brought to the *chambrée* state by heating in a wet pan for a few seconds. The odor of heart cooking brings a cat out from wherever he is.

The smaller hearts (lamb or veal) are treated the same way. They always seem to have more fat and gristle than the family-size ones, so do a lot of cutting and trimming before shoving them into your grinder. Gristle can't do your grinder much good and certainly doesn't impress a cat.

KIDNEYS

Kidneys are among the things considered to be "too good for a cat." Once a thing gets into the Escoffier cookbook, its price rises with its reputation. You would know that the *most* expensive kidney of all, lamb, appeals to a cat more than any of the others. You buy them by ones, twos, or threes, but there are times when there are more lamb kidneys than people who like them, so be patient. They can be quite reasonable. I must caution you, *never tell an Italian or Frenchman* that you are buying a kidney for a cat! He would *not* understand such extravagance, but we do, don't we?

LITTLE KIDNEYS (*Petits Rognons* or *Piccoli Rognoni*)

The Marquise Lili G——, who gave me this recipe, cautioned me to omit white wine, the shallots, the orégano, and butter when cooking them for a cat. Otherwise, they are exactly as she does them for her guests at her villa in Ischia.

METHOD: Allow lamb kidneys to wallow in boiling water for 10 minutes. This will take the chill from them and bring them to a medium rare state. Rinse them in cool water to make them easier to handle, then cut them into julienne strips, and again into tiny cubes.

Lamb kidneys are so delicious, they should be fed gradually. You know what happens when a cat likes something too much, and it would be a shame to have wasted all that cutting.

KIDNEYS (*Rognons*)

Large or small, a kidney is a kidney. Beef and veal kidneys are prepared in the same way, except that they contain a maximum of fat which should be cut away before the hot-water treatment, or you'll find yourself with enough soup for an army. Cutting a large kidney is a helter-skelter kind of mess, but, in the end, you'll have your strips and pieces and a drooling cat.

HALF AND HALF (*Moitié-Moitié* or *Mezzo-Mezzo*)

Half fresh kidney mixed with half canned kidney pleases cats. Half chopped kidney and half chopped heart makes them purr with gratitude.

SUGGESTIONS: On a busy day, remove all fat from a beef or veal kidney, throw it into the meat grinder, and grind away. *Chambrée* over boiling water until medium rare.

LIVER

Beef, baby beef, calf's, lamb's, and chicken livers all supply cats with darned good eating. Lamb liver is the least expensive, therefore is least appreciated by cats. Beef, baby beef, and calf's liver are in the higher brackets, but my *tripier* in Paris taught me a little secret. Thrifty French housewives, low on francs, but highly imaginative, buy what is called *les bouts de foie* (ends of liver, freely translated). Actually, these are the trimmings of expensive livers when muscles and sinews are cut away with nice big juicy areas of meat attached to them. The butcher sells them as waste for less than half the cost of liver by the slice. You can get a lot of trimmings in a pound, but beware of the unscrupulous butcher who adds the skin.

Before we serve liver to a cat we must know whether to cook it or leave it raw. Circumstances should color our decision. Raw liver has laxative qualities; cooked liver just the reverse. Some cats never *need* it raw; others should never have it cooked. I told you that a decision would have to be made.

Liver can be served in many ways, even raw. Raw liver shouldn't be *exactly* raw. When given the merest wallow in boiling water, it begins to turn white around the edges. Inside it is indeed a medium rare, on the raw side. Liver in this condition must be cut into pieces and served at once. (It cuts nicely after the hot-water treatment. All the slipperiness seems to leave.)

CHOPPED LIVER (*Foie Haché*)

Cook the liver until it is firm. Ten minutes should do the trick. Put it into the meat grinder. What comes out when you turn the crank is pure unadulterated chopped liver. It can be eaten as is or mixed with a canned cat food. It doesn't matter how unpalatable the canned food is. Once your chopped liver is added, bygones will be bygones.

PÂTÉ MAISON (*Chopped liver with some added attractions*)

Proceed as for *Foie Haché* but add about a tablespoon of soybean oil and a soupçon of salt. The soybean oil does wonderful things to the stomach machinery besides adding a few extra vitamins. For very young cats, just beginning to learn that Life Can Be Beautiful via liver, add the prescribed dose of cod-liver oil or brewer's yeast. You can get away with anything in liver.

Caution: A dish of my *Pâté Maison* in your refrigerator may confuse your husband or your guests. It *looks* as though it goes well with a martini. Label it *For Cats Only*.

MELT (*Rate de Boeuf* or *Milza*)

These fancy names are just another way of saying spleen. This glandlike ductless organ is situated near the stomach of men and animals and does something to the blood as it passes through. It has a reputation, too, of being the source of mirth, courage, ill humor, and spite—according to fable and adage. This amusing innard is about a yard long in cows and no more than three inches in lambs. All varieties (including your own, I suppose) are terribly slippery and spoil rapidly.

Cutting melt requires a good sharp knife and a lot of patience. There is a scissor-cutting school, too, but I have found that method very unsatisfactory. To begin with, we must toughen that ghastly membrane that covers the melt. Boiling water poured over it helps, but it has a tendency to shrink the darned thing. Never mind, just cut into the thing, which should be firm by now, and remove it. Once *that* is off, cutting up the stuff is a cinch. *Do not grind* melt!

When you have cut as much melt as I have, you, too, will be able to determine which in the butcher's case is for *you*. Leave the limp thin melt for the Hungarians, who will do it with paprika. You choose the thick one with an outer coating of fat, for cats. Don't be afraid to sniff it. "Teched" melt has an aroma like nothing else in the world, except perhaps an unburied rat.

Once the membrane is toughened, any good sharp[1] knife will remove it. Now, cut away. Slice, dice it, but never grind it, unless you want a mess of bloody membranes.

Dr. Fernand Méry, the noted French veterinary (and author of *Her Majesty the Cat*) wants a cat to have *no* offal but heart. He discourages the use of melt, so if you have your own doubts consult your veterinary. Cats seem to love it and, if melt has no way of doing any good, it certainly can't do any harm. *Warning:* if what you find in your cat's box after he has eaten melt frightens you, do not rush him to his physician. He is not having an internal hemorrhage! It's just that melt looks *odd* on the way out.

LUNG (*Poumon* or *Polmone*)

Lung is a staple in continental cat feeding. You get a lot for your money. Seeing it hanging from hooks in the *triperies* of Paris and Rome is hardly an attractive sight. Frankly, I can't bear to touch it, but then I'm *not* a cat. If your cat must have it, then simply boil it until it's firm enough to handle and cut. It can be served raw, too, but what a bloody mess that would make. In many households, feeding lung to pussy cats helps to balance the budget.

BRAINS

Every once in a while somebody makes a great discovery. Marie Curie did it with radium, Pasteur with rabies, Bell, the telephone— but my veterinary, Dr. Michael Miller, claims to have found the solution to cat constipation. *Brains.* Calf's brains, to be specific. I

---

[1] When I say sharp, I mean sharp sharp, almost razor-blade sharp.

can't prove that it works, but if you'd like to try, here's how you do it:

Get a calf brain somewhere and follow the instructions in Monsieur Escoffier's cookbook, which are:

Soak the brain in cold water, to cover, for an hour. Remove the membrane, then cook slowly in boiling salted water for a few minutes until that well-known gray matter turns white. Cool, then separate into small segments.

Escoffier suggests many of his sauces to use with brains, but we stop right here. Cats have no palate for Béchamel or Béarnaise. Perhaps they'll have no palate for the brains either, but then you can always eat them yourself.

MEATS

The meat world is large and nourishing. Meat can mean beef, lamb, mutton, veal, or horse. Pork is unsuitable for cats (and people). Not enough cooking can make it unfit for food; too much cooking takes the flavor away; served raw, it is dangerous. Let's leave it out of a cat's diet. There are so many other wonders in the world.

Perhaps the most natural way to feed a cat is to get a 2-pound porterhouse and let him gnaw his way through. At the present market price even the least expensive cuts of meats are too prohibitive to feed to a cat unless, of course, you shop on the Via della Croce, Rome, or the Rue de Buci, Paris. There they slice round steak "the other way," which allows you to buy it in slices of a half pound to a pound (250 grammes or a half kilo). I found most cuts of beef to be much cheaper than kidney abroad, but in the States the least expensive cut is chuck. Make it "the leaner the better" for all meats served to cats—and never, never buy it ground. Don't even grind it yourself. Ground meat is a waste of time. Most cats hate it because it sticks to the roofs of their mouths. In any case, you'll be depriving him of a good old-fashioned chew if meat is served premasticated.

BIFTECK TARTARE (*Steak Tartar*)

The chefs at Dominique's Restaurant on Rue Brea in Paris agree me that cats will relish this one. It's almost like their famous entree with only a few deletions:

½ pound stewing meat or chuck or any red-blooded beef or
lamb

1 raw egg

1 soupçon of a pinch of garlic salt

Cut the meat into large bite-size pieces. Beat egg until yolk and
white blend, then mix well into the meat. Add the garlic salt and
serve, *chambréed,* of course.

BOEUF SUMATRA (*Sumatra Meat*)

This is a variation on the method of feeding the Sumatra tigers
in the London Zoo. Ours is the domestic version for the "Tiger in
Your House."

Cut ½ pound beef into small cubes—or ask your butcher to
do it for *your* stew. Serve on a large dinner plate spaced 2 inches
apart[2] with a knuckle bone in the center.[3]

RABBIT

Most English cats live almost exclusively on rabbit, but you know
what English food is like. I've never cooked rabbit, touched it while
it was dead, or eaten it, but that means nothing, because I have
some very odd eating habits. From what I saw of London cats, rabbit seems to agree with them.

I asked Kay Walsh how she prepares it for her cat. "Darling, you
get a bunny at Harrod's, disjoint it, and put it into a pot with some
water, a few carrots, a leek, and a branch of parsley. When it's
finished, darling, it's soft, you know, like chicken. Then serve it
with some of the broth just like they do at the Ivy, in a divine
Wedgwood dish."

[2] I've been toying with the idea that especially *good* food is bolted. This, as we
know, results in an unfortunate upheaval. My charlady in London told me about
the big-plate idea. "You see, ducks," said she, "if you spread it about it takes longer
to eat. They go looking for their eats tidy like and it keeps the floor that way too."
[3] Bones: I *will not* give a chicken bone to *my* cat, but I will let him lick one that
is hard to handle. A knuckle bone with shreds of meat attached to it is perfectly safe.
Cats work hard at getting the flesh off and by that time are too bored to go after the
rest of it. Unlike dogs, cats never bury bones in sofas and under beds. The bone of
a leg of lamb is a perfect example of the sort of thing cats like. They do nothing
but lick and that is what tigers do.

FISH AND SEA FOOD

If you want your cat to love you, offer him a shore dinner. The *fruits de mer*—oysters, clams, mussels, crab, lobster, and shrimp, all without shells or sauce—make excellent cat food. The only thing that stands in the way is their price—too good for a cat.

I don't advise a dozen blue points on the half shell or *moules marinières* as a casual lunch dish, but bits of lobster, clam, and shrimp, put aside while preparing a spectacular casserole, could make some pussy cat mighty happy. Most likely your cat will be at your elbow while you are cracking crab or deveining or shelling shrimp. If nobody is looking, give him some. Cats are funny about goodies. I doubt whether any cat would like a full plate of shrimp or a lobster on the half shell, but they do like it as a snack once in a while just for the hell of it.

Some cats eat raw goldfish and even catfish right out of ponds, but whatever swims has to be cooked and boned before it's served to a cat.

Frozen fish, filleted by some faraway Nova Scotian or Icelander, offers an easy way out. Cod and haddock fillets are the least expensive of the lot. Cats love them.

Fish, unfortunately, pound for pound, does not have the filling power of meat, once inside the cat. Where a pound of meat might serve four meals, a pound of fish serves two, but it may be combined with other things and therefore be worth its weight in gold.

Frozen fish packages usually have cooking directions on the back of the wrapper. Cats like their fish unadorned, so omit the Béchamel sauces and white grapes. One of the best methods of cooking fish for cats is to poach it in water *in the oven*. Oven poaching, for some reason, keeps the fish smell confined behind closed doors, allowing the house to smell a little fresher than Fisherman's Wharf. It is also a safety measure. Cats are so impatient once they smell what's cooking, they sometimes try to get a paw into the boiling pot to hurry it along.

OVEN-POACHED FISH

Use a thawed, partially thawed, or fully frozen fillet (or fillets). Turn the oven to hot or about 400 degrees. Put the block of fish into an oven-proof loaf pan that just fits. Add water to cover and put it into the oven. Forget about it for 20 minutes, if your fish is thawed, or 35 to 40 minutes if it was still frozen. At the end of that period, open the oven door and remove it. It will be thoroughly cooked, white and flaky, and you had very little to do. If it is to be served immediately and it usually is, with a slotted spoon break off what is needed and run it under cold water. When it is cool enough to handle, ignore the pleadings of your cat and start to look for any bone a fish filleter may have overlooked. You'd be amazed at how many are left in. When you are sure that all is clear, you may serve it to the cat.

Fish may be oven-poached in milk, too. This is a "human" way of doing the same thing and the cat may like it and even decide to drink the milk, which by this time is as fishy as the fish itself. All fish should be sniffed, even the frozen kind. Very often a market defrosting its freezer will forget that fish is temperamental and doesn't like to thaw and be refrozen. Fish subjected to this treatment doesn't hesitate to tell you so. Throw it down the garbage disposer, but save the wrapper. You're entitled to a refund.

Freshly cooked fish can make any canned cat food more tempting. It's especially good with canned tuna, which can be quite a bore if served too regularly. Mixing one third freshly cooked fish with two thirds of a can of cat tuna gives it a new lease on life.

BOUILLABAISSE

Fish shops sell a chowder assortment that is made up of bits and pieces (some mysterious) of the denizens of the deep. This mélange, in which you can identify heads, tails, fins, and ends, is inexpensive and quite good. Its only drawback is its bones. If you've ever eaten a proper *bouillabaisse* or a *zuppa di pesce*, you know what I mean. Cat *bouillabaisse* does not contain oil or white wine, or saffron or French bread. It's just fish and water boiled to make beautiful music together. Treat your cat to 2 pounds of chowder assortment, because by the time you're through separating edible from inedible parts and have removed the bones you'll have only about half of what you started with. If you like you can add a *bouquet garni* in the form of a leek. Cats like leeks and leeks like cats.

Once the fish is cooked (this can be accomplished by the oven method too), cool it naturally or artificially, and start your search for bones, tails, fins, etc. What's left will be enough to satisfy any cat.

Under the fish heading, among the *don't serves* are: herring, salted or pickled, caviar, finnan haddie, kippers, anchovies, or smoked salmon. It's not the fish that we don't want our cats to eat, it's the salt, spices, and smoking preparations they come with.

Domestic sardines (called Maine sardines) canned in soy oil are a good addition to a fish dinner. Mix or match with equal amounts of canned cat food—either all tuna or one made with a fish base. Cats may not object to mixing fish with kidney or liver, but I do.

Inexpensive canned salmon or jack mackerel ought to be in everyone's cat larder for emergencies.

VEGETABLES

Of all things, cats love corn on the cob, either raw or slightly cooked. They will love you forever if you put a teaspoon of freshly scraped corn into their food. They will crown you Queen of the May if you are imaginative enough to give them a whole ear of corn to chew and gnaw as a bone. It's good for them, too, as a hair ball chaser and as a gentle persuader in the intestinal tract.

A lot of people find vegetables hard to take, so don't blame a cat too much if he says, "I say it's spinach and I say to hell with it!" I would give up trying to force-feed a cat vegetables. "Eat it or else" tactics won't get you anywhere and may make your cat distrust anything put in front of him.

Try your cat on mashed carrots. When I say *mashed,* I mean *mashed* to within an inch of their lives. Stir the mess (I mean mess) into something he loves best and he *may* eat them. You have to consider the fact that he may *not,* too. Sometimes a dab of soft butter added to carrots makes them a little more interesting. I know that they always seem so to me.

Cooked leeks[4] (one of the more elegant relations of the onion family) add a continental touch to an ordinary dish of canned food. Like leek, cooked endive, though expensive, is an excellent stomach cleanser. The French boil their leeks and endive until tender, drain, and pass them through a *moulin*.[5] Added to a cat's dinner, they say these vegetables do wonderful things for hair balls.

The French, who are forever adding butter to everything, put it into a cat's food too. A teaspoon of soft butter mixed into anything makes it taste better and greases the machinery.

[4] The water in which your leeks are cooked is precious. Do as the Parisiennes do. Use it as a base for your own *potages* or drink a glass of it once in a while. It does glorious things to your skin by cleansing your liver. It's a secret given to me a long time ago by Lady Mendl (Elsie de Wolfe).

[5] A food mill. Every Frenchman has one!

And, to make it even easier for you, here's a suggested week's menu:

MONDAY

BRUNCH

Ricotta Dorata

DINNER

Bifteck Tartare

TUESDAY

BRUNCH

Pâté Maison

DINNER

Poached cod
Raw corn cut from cob—
in season
Water

WEDNESDAY

Vaseline—an hour before brunch

BRUNCH

Lamb kidneys

DINNER

Canned tuna fish mixed
with cooked leeks

THURSDAY

BRUNCH

Lait d'Enfance with Pablum, cooked cereal, or soaked puppy biscuits

DINNER

Bouts de foie—raw or cooked

FRIDAY

BRUNCH

Ground heart

DINNER

Bouillabaisse

SATURDAY

BRUNCH

Moitié-Moitié (kidney and heart)

DINNER

Canned salmon

SUNDAY

BRUNCH

Boeuf Sumatra

DINNER

Chicken skins with cooked mashed endive
Bits of shrimp and crab meat
Saucer of cream

BON APPETIT!